WEAPON

GERMAN MACHINE GUNS OF WORLD WAR I

STEPHEN BULL

Series Editor Martin Pegler

First published in Great Britain in 2016 by Osprey Publishing,
PO Box 883, Oxford, OX1 9PL, UK
1385 Broadway, 5th Floor, New York, NY 10018, USA
E-mail: info@ospreypublishing.com

Osprey Publishing, part of Bloomsbury Publishing Plc

A CIP catalogue record for this book is available from the British
Library

Print ISBN: 978 1 4728 1516 3
PDF ebook ISBN: 978 1 4728 1517 0
ePub ebook ISBN: 978 1 4728 1518 7

Index by Rob Munro
Typeset in Sabon and Univers
Originated by PDQ Media, Bungay, UK
Printed in China through World Print Ltd.

16 17 18 19 20   10 9 8 7 6 5 4 3 2 1

Osprey Publishing supports the Woodland Trust, the UK's leading
woodland conservation charity. Between 2014 and 2018 our
donations are being spent on their Centenary Woods project in
the UK.

www.ospreypublishing.com

Glossary

Abteilung	department, detachment or section
Ausbildungsvorschrift	training provision, or instruction
Auslöser	trigger or release
Dampfrohr	steam tube or pipe
Dreibein or *Dreifuß*	tripod
Einheitsmaschinengewehr	universal machine gun
Felddienst	field service
Flugbahn	trajectory or flight path
Gewehrprüfungskommission	Rifle Test Commission
Gurt	belt
Gurtfüller	belt loader or filler
Kasten	box, chest or receiver
Kastendeckel	box lid, receiver cover
Korn	sight 'bead' (also 'grain')
Lauf	barrel, as in 'gun barrel'
Lehrkursus	training course
Mantel	jacket
Mantelpanzer	armoured jacket
Maschinengewehr	machine gun
Maschinengewehr-Kompagnie	machine-gun company
Maschinengewehrtruppen	machine-gun troops
Patronen	cartridges
Rückstoßverstärker	recoil, or muzzle, booster
Schild	shield
Schießgestelle	gun mount (literally 'shooting stand')
Schießvorschrift	shooting provision or instruction
Schlitten	sled
Schloß	lock
Schloßhebel	lock lever, crank handle
Sperrklinke	pawl or ratchet
Trommel	drum
Unterrichtsbuch	instruction book
Visier	sight
Visierlinie	line of sight
Waffenmeister	armourer
Zielfernrohr	telescopic or optical sight
Zuführer	feed

Acknowledgements

My real introduction to the 'Devil's Paintbrush' was in the 1980s,
when Dolf Goldsmith visited the weapons department of the
National Army Museum to undertake research for the debut
edition of his ground-breaking book of the same name. Dolf
sparked my interest in Maxim's guns, and so to him is due the
greatest thanks. Since then, and like many others, I am much
indebted to the late Herbert Woodend, formerly of the old MoD
'Pattern Room'; also to Mark Murray-Flutter of the Royal
Armouries at Leeds; and Fergus Read and the team at what was,
until recently, the Department of Exhibits and Firearms at the
Imperial War Museum, London. I cannot also fail to mention
Colonel John Downham and Jane Davies at the Lancashire
Infantry Museum, who helped bring together a group of no fewer
than four MG 08s and MG 08/15s as part of the World War I
display in the Museum of Lancashire, Preston.

Editor's note

Unless otherwise noted, the illustrations in this volume are drawn
from the collection of the author. Metric measurements are used
in this book. For ease of comparison please refer to the following
conversion table:

1km = 0.62 miles
1m = 1.09yd / 3.28ft / 39.37in
1cm = 0.39in
1mm = 0.04in
1kg = 2.20lb
1g = 0.04oz / 15.43 grains

Front cover, above: MG 08/15 with drum magazine and muzzle
booster, c.1918 (© Royal Armouries PR.7307). Below: MG 08
with Saxon infantry gun team, c.1916. The belt feeds from a
single-belt 250-round box; in the foreground are two 500-round
Modell 1911 boxes, each designed for two 250-round belts. The
gun loader wears a leather 'dragging strap' around his shoulder
for manhandling the gun.
Title page: A Bavarian NCO with an MG 08 on a light anti-
aircraft tripod mount, working from a pit, c.1918. The
500-round ammunition box has been crudely marked with a 'K',
denoting that the rounds are armour-piercing. The gunner aims
using the flip-up 'iron' sight; suitable adjustment of the mount
would also allow engagement of ground targets.

CONTENTS

INTRODUCTION

'In a moment the gun was in order and began to bark,' recalled Georg Bucher of his time on the Verdun battlefield.

An early-production and now very battered MG 08 built by DWM in front-line service, *c.*1916. Its 'trench mount' is a small tripod clamped to the water jacket, sprung so as to be flipped up and down quickly.

Gaaten pulled ammunition belts from the cases which Sonderbeck held ready for him. Tak tak tak tak tak tak ... we trembled with blood lust and fury as we mowed them down. Rows of them fell at a time but still the sky blue flood came nearer ... tak tak tak tak tak ... 'The crowd on

the right!' Riedel screamed. The barrel of the gun moved to the right, my eyes, which were as inflamed and blood thirsty as Riedel's, followed the sights. Such were the Verdun battles ... Tak tak tak tak tak tak. The crowd dissolved in blood and death. Sonderbeck pushed a heap of empty cartridge cases out of the way. Riedel thrust a fresh belt into place, while Gaaten had another in readiness. Tak tak tak ... Would it never end? (Bucher 2005: 51–52)

If ever there was a weapon requiring its own biography, it is the one nicknamed the 'Devil's Paintbrush' – the Maxim machine gun of World War I; and of all those Maxims, deployed by many different countries, it is the German MG 08 which stands head and shoulders above all others — if not in terms of technical development, then at least on account of its importance to the war on the Western Front, and by extension the war in general. For, along with artillery and the trench, it was arguably the machine gun that made German strategy, and four-year survival, possible. With the failure of the Schlieffen Plan in the first months of the war, machine guns became crucial to defence in the West. This would remain the case throughout much of the conflict. Moreover, with the passage of time and shortages of manpower, automatic weapons became ever more important as part of a defensive plan, being used in progressively more subtle ways.

With the advent of a lighter version of the MG 08, in the shape of the 08/15, the German Maxim would attain a new lease of life, being not only able to take on a more flexible role in the front line, but to be carried in

A typical battlefield MG 08 team, 1917. The gunner and loader are directed by an NCO commander, who would usually have been located a few metres from the weapon where he could both take cover and observe the impact of rounds. The two ammunition numbers, far left and right, would take cover further back or to the side, ready to give close support with the grenades and carbine evident here. Four men wear *Tragegurten* ('dragging straps'), and all five the *Stahlhelm* ('steel helmet').

An American soldier encounters an MG 08, still steaming and with its top cover knocked off, on a German street, 1945. This weapon has been modified during the interwar period by the addition of a squeeze trigger, this being easier to operate than the original 'thumb' trigger.

the forefront of the attack. At the end of the war an air-cooled 08/18 commenced production. Nor was this all: with relatively minor modification, the MG 08 would also be deployed in fortresses, against aircraft, with mountain troops and in tanks. In the shape of the LMG 08 the gun was taken aloft above the battlefields in the Fokker and Albatros flying machines.

While the MG 08 was progressively overtaken by new generations of weapons from the latter part of World War I onwards, it did not simply disappear from the inventory with the collapse of Imperial Germany. It survived as a front-line infantry arm into the 1930s, and though theoretically supplanted or superseded successively by the MG 13, MG 34 and finally the MG 42, remained in use with some German forces through to 1945. Internationally, MG 08 and commercial variants continued to be used in a variety of countries including the Netherlands, Poland, and Lithuania. Some were supplied to China, which also produced its own Type 24 machine gun under licence, a weapon that saw action in Korea, and which in its turn was supplied to countries including Malaysia, Indonesia, and even North Vietnam which used it during the Vietnam War. The MG 08 and its successors therefore had a combat life spanning half a century.

For the German soldier the relationship between man and gun was definitely one of love and hate: the brutal precision machine that saved the line and cut down thousands of the enemy was also an unforgiving beast – and a potentially difficult mistress. Like the humans serving it, the MG 08 required water and feeding, and shelter from the elements and shells alike. It was heavy to carry and wearing on the hands and shoulders; often it was too hot to handle easily, and if not tended properly could simply give up. At such a crucial moment, as Bucher records, the crew might be forced to flee ignominiously, or resort to the use of pistols, grenades and entrenching tools. Often the machine-gunners did not run, and indeed tended to be left until last, covering their comrades, and were all too frequently left to their fate.

DEVELOPMENT
The 'Devil's Paintbrush'

MAXIM AND HIS GUN

The issue German MG 08, and its lighter and even more widely distributed offspring the 08/15, were just two of the many variants of 'Maxim' machine gun. The Maxim was certainly not the first 'repeating' weapon, nor the first to have a mechanical method of reloading; but it was the first to harness the power of discharge and recoil to perform 'automatic' reloading, and therefore the first true 'machine' gun. With some justification its action has been compared to that of an internal-combustion engine whose 'strokes' are powered by the firing of the cartridges. To operate the Maxim after the chambering and firing of a first round required no more human intervention than to keep a trigger depressed. There was no hand cranking of the type associated with the famous gun invented by Dr Richard Jordan Gatling, nor any lever pulling, as needed to keep Gardner or Nordenfelt weapons in action.

The inventor, Hiram Stevens Maxim (1840–1916), was American of English and French Huguenot descent. His first US patent of 1866 had been for 'irons for curling hair', but thereafter he moved onto mills, engines, dynamos and electric lights. At the end of his life *Who's Who* would describe Maxim as 'a civil, mechanical and electrical engineer', known for his experiments with heavier-than-air flight, and his scientific papers. In a lecture to the London Institution of Mechanical Engineers, Maxim claimed that he first considered the possibility of mechanically recharged weapons in his teens, when working together with his father, as early as the mid-1850s. Nevertheless the idea that harnessing recoil could be the key to a new system occurred to him only after the American Civil War, when some former combatants gave him the opportunity to fire their

Springfield rifled muskets. The heavy kick accompanying discharge came as dramatic evidence of the hitherto wasted energy generated by just a single shot. Similar observations had been reported to the Royal Society as long ago as the 17th century, though Maxim may have been unaware of them.

Whatever the inspiration, Maxim did little to develop his notions until after he moved to England in 1881: here he conducted experiments, culminating in his first gun patent of 1883. In this a Model 1873 Winchester was converted by means of springs and a bolt to throw out the empty cartridge after firing and re-cock the hammer. This was followed swiftly by work on magazine feed, and other gun patents. In 1884 and 1885 he devised both sliding breech mechanisms which ejected and reloaded, and a top-mounted radial cartridge magazine, versions of which would appear in other weapons. In 1885 he unveiled what was later popularly known as his 'transitional' machine gun, with perfected toggle-lock mechanism, distinctive brass water jacket, belt feed and multi-function extractor. This took a gold medal at the International Inventions Exhibition, South Kensington, and a larger version duly became the 1in 'Pom Pom' gun – a weapon Albert Vickers thought so deadly that the British Government would be well advised to buy it, and keep secret from foreign powers.

Work continued apace during 1886 and 1887, with further patents covering sliding breech action, hydraulic buffers, return springs, turning

A Landsturm infantryman, wearing the distinctive oilcloth cap, stands guard over an MG 01 on an early-type sled mount at Paderborn, c.1914. The weapon feeds from a 250-round box and has a cylindrical water can to the right.

bolts, barrel manufacture and ammunition feeds. By now all the essentials were in place, and Maxim himself regarded tests conducted in Switzerland in 1887 as an important turning point. He was accompanied by Albert Vickers and a weapon was fired in competition with a Gardner gun at ranges up to 1,200m, most notably against a target intended to represent an artillery battery. The adjudicators concluded that by firing 333 rounds, in three bursts, the Maxim would have devastated the battery.

It is significant to note that the advance of Maxim's work was materially aided by the French development of smokeless powder in 1884, loaded in reliable, solid-drawn, centrefire, metallic cartridges, themselves of uniform quality and of a size small enough to allow large numbers to be fed smoothly and rapidly through the mechanism of a weapon. Where good cartridges were available the Maxim usually performed well; and the 'little gun' was itself now of a size to be handled effectively by a couple of crewmen, and once loaded, discharged by only one. On the business front, another notable step forward was the amalgamation of the Maxim and Nordenfelt companies in 1887–88, upon which new shares were issued, and the way cleared to introduce to market what Maxim was pleased to call the 'World Standard' machine gun. A concerted sales drive and charm offensive followed, with Maxim himself demonstrating considerable showmanship in conducting test firings. Very quickly, small numbers of guns were sold to the UK War Office and the Italian and French governments. Samples were also sold as far afield as the Congo and other parts of Africa, the Netherlands, Spain, Argentina and Singapore. A few were even picked up privately by forward-thinking gentlemen serving with British Volunteer units.

'German Insect powder for Nico-lice': Russian Tsar Nicholas II sprayed with bullets by an MG 99 team, as depicted in an early World War I propaganda postcard. The artist may not have fully appreciated the Maxim mechanism, as the gunner appears to be working the cocking handle as a firing crank. In reality the cocking handle was usually operated twice only for loading, the weapon then firing automatically on depression of the trigger.

GERMAN ADOPTION AND MANUFACTURE

Perhaps oddly, sales to Germany were slow at first, and an attempted alliance between Maxim and the growing industrial arms giant Krupp, the aim of which was a 20-year agreement for manufacture, made little progress, though Krupp did pay royalties on some larger 'Pom Pom' guns. The Kaiser saw the machine gun in 1888 and as a result was moved to purchase (from his own pocket) a few of the 'World Standard' Maxims, in 11mm calibre; one was made available to each of the two *Garde-Dragoon-Regimenter*. Official firing trials were conducted by the German Rifle Commission at Zorndorf in 1889. That same year a single example 'adapted to the German cartridge' was also requested by the 'verbal order' of a German admiral, through an agent in Italy. This was delivered in November, at the then vast sum of £284 14s.

According to Hiram Maxim's own account, a real breakthrough came in Germany when Kaiser Wilhelm II visited Spandau, together with Edward, Prince of Wales and other guests, for a demonstration of four of the leading repeating weapons of the day:

> Three hundred and thirty-three rounds were to be fired from each gun at a large target at a range of two hundred metres. The old Gatling gun was worked by four men, and got through the cartridges in a little less than a minute. The same number of men fired the same number of rounds in the Gardner gun in a little over a minute. The Nordenfelt was also fired and did just about the same. Then one man advanced, took his seat on the trail of the Maxim gun, touched a button and 333 cartridges went off in less than half a minute. They examined the targets and found that the hand worked guns had made bad targets because the guns themselves had participated in the action of the lever or crank. All the projectiles from the Maxim gun were in the bull's-eye and the whole centre of it had been shot away. The Emperor walked back, examined the gun, and placing his finger on it, said: 'That is the gun – there is no other'. (Maxim 1915: 208–10)

So excited was Wilhelm that he also fired the Maxim himself, inadvertently traversing towards the General Staff. Maxim was forced to intervene to prevent a spectacular accident.

As well as the enthusiasm of the Kaiser, Maxim was fortunate enough to enlist influential shareholders to his newly enlarged company, including Lord Rothschild who had very useful German connections. In 1891, negotiations commenced with Ludwig Lowe of Berlin for the manufacture of guns to satisfy the German market, and at least seven additional guns in 8mm calibre found their way to Germany that year. In 1892 a seven-year agreement was drawn up under which Maxim took orders and payments, and furnished Lowe with the necessary working drawings. When weapons were paid for Lowe would be remunerated for cost of materials and wages, plus an additional 150 per cent on the wages. A special clause noted that Krupp might also make Maxim machine guns for the German government – but that in the event this option was ever exercised Maxim retained the right to set the price, and undertook to split the profits with Lowe. These arrangements being in place, an order promptly materialized from the German Navy, which received its first consignment of Maxim guns from Lowe in 1894. Thereafter manufacture was firmly established in Berlin, and Lowe, formerly known for production of other machinery, formed a new subsidiary from its existing munitions staff under the title Deutsche Waffen- und Munitionsfabriken, or DWM, in 1896. This made commercial sense, but it has been said that this was done in order to make the company sound more German and less Jewish at a time of growing anti-Semitism. With the end of the contract with Maxim in 1898 DWM took on new orders from Austria, Argentina, Switzerland and Russia.

When the German Navy adopted the Maxim there was already a clear rationale for its deployment. Its utility in colonial warfare had been demonstrated, and it had roles in use from the decks of ships, and with shore parties where powerful defensive fire could help make up for small numbers of men. On board ships the Maxim was used from a turning pedestal, ashore it was used with a tripod mount. On the other hand, and despite the encouragements of the Kaiser, the German Army had as yet little notion as to what it might be supposed to do with the Maxim gun. During the Franco-Prussian War (1870–71), carriage-mounted, hand-cranked, multi-shot weapons had been used essentially as a species of light artillery, and so it was that sample Maxims were first sent by Prussian War Minister Bronsart von Schellendorf to the artillery to determine their use. None was readily identified, though as with artillery pieces it was soon decided that Maxims should be provided with horses and full-sized wooden-wheeled carriages, at least for longer-distance transport. Experiments with the *Jäger* light infantry only commenced in 1898, and these were not universally successful given problems with overheating and jamming, and the important question of whether Maxims should be deployed individually or in groups. Other formations – including the Garde-Korps, I. Armeekorps and XVI. Armeekorps – conducted further

German marines prepare to carry a naval Maxim Model 1894 'over the top' near Albert, 1918. The brass-barrelled MG 94 was not fitted with a sled mount, instead using this distinctive tripod for land service.

trials in 1899. The recommendation then was that Maxims should be kept in six-gun batteries, so a group could continue to function even if one of its weapons was out of action. Voices were also raised in favour of the deployment of machine guns with cavalry, with the influential German staff officer and military theorist Friedrich von Bernhardi, Chief of Staff of XVI. Armeekorps, arguing in his 1899 work *Unsere Kavallerie im nächsten Kriege* (*Our Cavalry in the Next War*) for an enlarged cavalry arm equipped not only with rifles, but directly supported with both artillery and machine guns. The result was that in time of war it was now planned that independent machine-gun detachments should march with the cavalry.

While tactical possibilities remained in flux, home-grown production of the German Maxim moved into a new phase with the appearance of the MG 99, purchased in small numbers from DWM by the German Army. The MG 99 differed from the naval type most significantly in that it had a new mounting to which the brass barrel jacket was attached by means of a clamp. The early version of this new *Schlittenlafette* or 'sled mount' had a large and distinctive 'handle and gear' elevating mechanism, and four feet. It could be folded, either completely for transport, or partially, in stages, to allow the weapon to be fired from different heights with the crew prone, seated or kneeling. Folded, the gun and mount were carried on a vehicle, or the back of a pack animal; it was also possible to drag the piece short distances. The barrel jacket clamping arrangement of the MG 99 proved less than ideal, and it was itself rapidly superseded by a modified type in 1901. In the MG 01, top- and bottom-mounted trunnions were fitted towards the rear of the barrel jacket, which was now of steel rather than brass.

The MG 01 was doubtless an improvement, and DWM obtained various overseas sales including those to Chile and Bulgaria. At about this time lightweight spoked wheels were fitted either side of the sled mount, permitting the equipment to be pulled or pushed by the crew. Such wheels certainly appear in photographs of guns sold to Bulgaria. This type of sled was described by Oberst Friedrich August Oscar von Merkatz (1876–1949) as the Schlitten 03. Yet promising as the latest model might have

Artist's colour postcard depicting a Prussian 'machine-gun detachment of the infantry' from the first decade of the 20th century. The guns are MG 99 types with the heavy 'handle and gear' elevating mechanism, and the crew wear dark-blue dress uniform. Though most of the weapons have been dismounted, one fires from the gun cart.

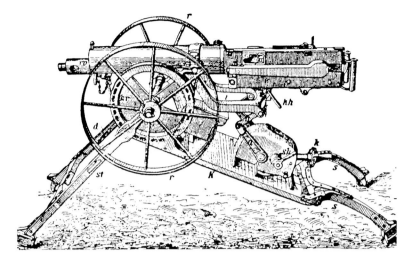

An early MG 01 of the type supplied by DWM to Chile, with spoked wheels integral to the sled mount. Note also the 'coffee mill' style elevating gear on the sled mount. Similar weapons also saw use by Bulgarian forces fighting on the German side during World War I, and in the bloody German campaign against the Herero people in South West Africa, 1904–07.

been, exercises with the German Army soon cast doubt on both organization and tactics. In an accurate prognostication the sled-mounted Maxim was criticized on grounds of both weight and mobility, and it was soon realized that there would be difficulty manoeuvring machine guns with the horse in wartime. A strong body of opinion among infantry and cavalry officers agreed that *Maschinengewehr-Abteilungen* or 'MG detachments' were best placed behind the front-line infantry, to be advanced no closer than 800m from the enemy position. The idea that Maxims would fight best in defensive groups may well have led offensively minded officers to underestimate the guns' potential. Nevertheless, by 1903 11 *Maschinengewehr-Abteilungen* were formed: 1. Garde, 2. Garde, 1. to 8., and 1. Bayerische. The newly formed detachments remained with the cavalry divisions during the great annual manoeuvres, during which their performance was unimpressive. In the manoeuvres of 1903 the Kaiser himself commanded a vast body of cavalry, supported by four artillery batteries and four machine-gun detachments. The cavalry was judged to have overrun the 'enemy' infantry, and the machine guns played little useful part. Later, the number of independent *Maschinengewehr-Abteilungen* rose to 16, by the addition of three in Alsace and Lorraine, and two in Saxony.

The tendency to regard the midst of the infantry, and fortresses, as the essential province of the machine gun, and the weapon itself merely as ancillary to other arms, would only be seriously disturbed by the Russo-Japanese War in 1904, where in the siege of Port Arthur conditions descended into trench warfare. As the *Militär-Wochenblatt* of June 1908 pointed out in glowing terms,

> The machine guns were extraordinarily successful. In the defence of entrenchments especially they had a most telling effect on the assailants at the moment of the assault. But they also were of service to the attack, being extremely useful in sweeping the crest of the defenders' parapets; as a few men can advance under cover with these weapons during an engagement, it is possible to bring them up without much

loss to a decisive point. The fire of six machine guns is equal to that of a battalion, and this is of enormous importance at the decisive moment and place. (Quoted in Longstaff & Atteridge 1917: 47)

Remarks such as this, plus the fact that the 'Russian' Maxims had been manufactured by DWM in Germany, could only feed speculation as to whether the German Army itself possessed enough machine guns. The Reichstag was approached for additional funding, but questions were asked by Socialist deputies who contested the perceived level of threat posed by French machine-gun procurement. A German Army aspiration for six guns per regiment was scaled back to a target of just six per brigade in 1907. This level of issue was yet to be achieved when the Moroccan Crisis of 1911 again led to demands for a more generous allocation, and eventually the Army Bill of 1912 acceded to the supply of six guns per regiment.

By this time the final model of Maxim to be introduced into the German Army prior to the outbreak of World War I had appeared: the MG 08. Complaints about the excessive weight of the MG 01 had not fallen entirely upon deaf ears, and it was on this matter that development focused. While the lock and basics of operation remained the same, DWM and the state arsenal at Spandau worked on replacing some of the heaviest parts with lightweight steel. The water jacket, trunnion block, feed block, fusee spring cover and backplate assemblies were all modified. The MG 08 was still heavy – at 22.2kg for the barrel assembly and 34.9kg for the sled, even without armour, ammunition or water – but a saving of about 7.7kg was achieved. Additionally, the size of the cocking-lever knob was marginally increased for better grip, and a bracket for mounting an optical sight was added. The sled mount was also reworked, without any integral wheels, resulting in a very stable, if bulky, platform. At the same time a large detachable crew shield was designed for the gun. Useful as this might have been under certain circumstances, actually carrying it around negated any weight savings, and unless dug in, the gun became even more obvious

Prussian guardsmen on exercise adopt a prone firing position with an MG 01, next to the gun wagon. Note the water can, and the early-type small 'ammunition sled' fitted for up to six end-opening ammunition boxes.

on the battlefield. After completion of modifications the new gun went into production at Spandau in 1908, and a sum of 14 million Marks was allotted for troop familiarization with machine guns. The gun, mount and shield were referred to officially as the Maschinengewehr 08, Schlitten 08 and Schild 08. DWM followed suit, producing the latest model from 1909.

With MG 08 series production under way and funding in place, the scheme for making an MG detachment available to each three-battalion infantry regiment became practical, with a six-gun *Maschinengewehr-Kompagnie* ('Machine Gun Company') progressively becoming a feature of each regiment. However, as late as the manoeuvres of 1912 British observers were still underwhelmed by numbers and performance:

> Machine guns appeared to play a somewhat minor role this year. The proportion of these guns to infantry is at present hardly large enough to make them very conspicuous. Six machine guns to 4,200 men ... are hardly an adequate number. On the evening of 11th September the Blue army was extended over a front of 30 kilometres, and along the whole of that front there were only eight machine gun companies. This state of affairs will be remedied in time. No new ideas as to the employment of these weapons appear to be prevalent. (General Staff no date: 53–54)

This situation would change dramatically, prompted first by stepping up production and issue, and then by the advent of war in 1914.

A souvenir montage of the *Maschinengewehr-Kompagnie* of Königlich Bayerisches 2. Infanterie-Regiment *Kronprinz*, founded at Munich in 1908. Depicted against the cityscape are two MG 08 teams; a rangefinder, a machine-gun cart, the armourers, officers, horses and the unit blacksmith at work. As of 1914 an MG company comprised six guns, four officers, 104 other ranks, 12 vehicles and about 43 horses.

THE MG 08 REVEALED

1. *Zielfernrohrfuß* (optical sight mount)
2. *Schraubdeckel mit Pinselhalter und Öl Pinsel* (screw cap with brush holder and oil brush)
3. *Handgriff* (hand grip)
4. *Behälter für Öl, Vaseline und kleinere Reserveteile* (containers for oil, Vaseline and small spares)
5. *Lederpolster* (leather pad)
6. *Haberad* (elevating wheel)
7. *Abzug* (trigger)
8. *Sicherung* (safety)
9. *Mantelpanzer* (armoured jacket)
10. *Federeinrichtung* (fusee spring cover)
11. *Kastendeckel* (receiver cover)
12. *Visier* (sight)
13. *Schlittenkufen* (sled runner)
14. *Dampfablaufschlauches* (steam outlet hose)
15. *Gewehrschlitten* (gun sled)
16. *Achsrohr* (axle tube / pivot)
17. *Schloßhebel* (lock lever / crank handle)
18. *Zuführer* (feed)
19. *Visierkorn* (sight bead)
20. *Rückstoßverstärker* (muzzle booster)
21. *Polster zum tragen* (carrying pad)
22. *Schloßbehälter* (lock container)
23. *Gurt* (belt)

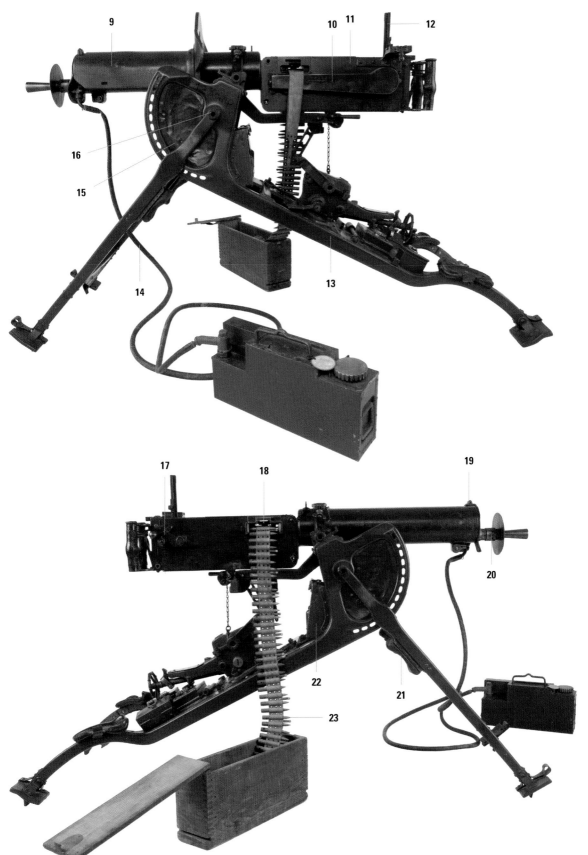

THE 'HEAVY' AND 'LIGHT' MACHINE GUN QUESTION

While the MG 08 was undoubtedly a good machine gun, meeting requirements and arguably proving to be only very marginally inferior on active service to guns produced a few years later, such as the Vickers, the advent of war identified new requirements it was ill placed to satisfy. Perhaps most crucially, though it was possible to carry the MG 08 forward in support of an attack, it was heavy and required time to set up. During 1915, experimentation with a variety of *Hilfslafette* ('auxiliary mount') types therefore began. These improvised small mountings were lighter than the sled and allowed more rapid deployment to and from bunkers and fire positions; and being less bulky, they were also less likely to attract attention. For obvious reasons they became known in English as 'trench mounts'.

Useful as they were, MG 08 trench mounts solved only part of the problem. For though a good deal of weight was saved by the omission of the sled, the mechanism and barrel unit were still heavy, and – being water cooled and belt fed – required water and separate boxes of ammunition. At the same time, the absence of the sturdy purpose-designed mount set limits to accuracy and reduced effective range. As British Intelligence noted in 1917:

> When the emergency carriage [trench mount] is used, the guns cannot usually fire more than 200 to 300 metres. This carriage can, therefore, only be used in places (especially in the front line trenches) situated at that distance from the targets in view. In any positions further to the rear, and in any intermediate positions, the sledge carriage must be used if the maximum range of the machine gun is to be employed. (General Staff 1917b: 2.23)

This was a relatively minor handicap in fixed defence, but problems were cruelly exposed when the enemy began to deploy 'automatic rifles' and

A *Scharfschützen* ('sharpshooter') team with their MG 08 on a wooden-board 'trench mount'. Identified by an oval machine-gun badge depicting an MG 08, worn on the left upper arm, the *Maschinengewehr-Scharfschützen* units were first formed from experienced personnel in early 1916. This group are wearing both the *Stahlhelm* and the Modell 1915 gasmask.

'light machine guns' in the attack, or if counter-attacks were needed. Ultimately, new light weapons lined up against German forces would include the Model 1909 Hotchkiss; the not very reliable French Chauchat and the Mle RSC 1917; and eventually the remarkable US Browning Automatic Rifle. However, one weapon above all others brought home to German High Command the fact that finding a solution to the problem was crucial. That weapon was the Lewis light machine gun. Like the other weapons mentioned, it had three features that made it more portable than the MG 08: it was air cooled; had a self-contained method of ammunition supply; and was considerably lighter, at 12.8kg unloaded. While not suitable for sustained-fire operation, still not particularly ergonomic and sometimes prone to stoppages, it was more reliable and practical than many of its contemporaries, and the British Army took delivery of increasing numbers during 1915. By the end of that year, clear tactical distinctions were being drawn between the Vickers, now placed in the hands of Britain's Machine Gun Corps, and the Lewis, which by mid-1916 was issued on a scale of two per company to front-line infantry. The German authorities were so impressed by the Lewis that not only were captured examples employed, but some were converted from .303in to take 7.92mm ammunition.

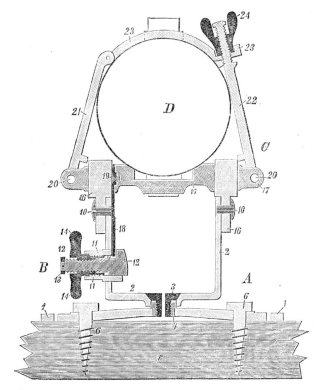

Die M.G.-Hilfslafette.

Bild 45.

Die M.G.-Hilfslafette

Diagram of the standard *Hilfslafette* for the MG 08 (Merkatz 1917 & 1918). This basic light 'trench mount' consisted of a steel ring and pivot for screwing down onto a variety of surfaces, such as a board or post. Relatively light and cheap, it improved the handiness of the gun, but was less stable than a sled or tripod.

Capture of a Lewis-gunner, late 1916 (overleaf)

Until the widespread issue of the MG 08/15, German infantry were short of light automatic weapons, and reliant upon modest numbers of stopgaps. The Danish Madsen, shown upper right with its distinctive 25-round box magazine, was one of the latter. *Musketen-Bataillone* armed with Madsens fought on the Somme in 1916, and some weapons were used later in the war. A Madsen team usually comprised four men with an immediate ammunition supply of 800 rounds in 32 magazines. With few spares and the difficulty of replacing Madsen guns, the capture of a Lewis gun to supplement resources was an extremely welcome event. In the foreground is an MG 08 on a simple 'trench mount', being prepared for stowage against weather and bombardment in a front-line shelter.

THE MG 08/15 AND COMPETING DESIGNS

While British and French offensives often foundered during 1915 and 1916, German reactions to the Lewis made it clear that a response was urgently required. As Generalleutnant Hermann von Stein – commander of XIV. Reservekorps, and of the Monchy–River Somme sector in July 1916 – reported of the Somme battle:

> The attack of the 1st July was well prepared and the [British] infantry was splendidly equipped with all kinds of weapons for close combat. It was provided with large numbers of Lewis guns which were brought into action very quickly and skilfully in newly captured positions. It is very desirable that our infantry should be equipped with a large number of light machine guns of this description in order to increase the intensity of its fire. (General Staff 1916a: 8)

Arguably, a German response was bedevilled by too many options, and in fact the Gewehrprüfungskommission had actually started its work on more mobile machine weapons well before the battle of the Somme. Certain guns were already to hand, but available only in painfully small numbers. Now there was not only the possible challenge of developing quickly an ideal 'niche' gun for the job, but also a far-sighted, if currently impractical, lobby in favour of the development of an *Einheitsmaschinengewehr*: a universal or 'one type' machine gun. If such a versatile weapon could be made to answer both 'light' and 'heavy' roles, it could become a general-purpose piece, keeping manufacture, deployment and training as simple and efficient as possible.

Key weapons considered included the Madsen, Parabellum, Dreyse, Bergmann, the new MG 16 and lightweight adaptations of the existing Maxim. The Danish-designed Madsen, produced well before the war, was regarded as an 'automatic rifle', recoil operated, with a hinged bolt, and a cyclic rate of about 450rds/min. Obtained both by captures from the Russians, and apparently by a small order from Denmark originally intended for Bulgaria, it was available relatively quickly and converted to 7.92mm calibre, if only in small numbers. As of the autumn of 1915, three so-called *Musketen-Bataillone* were created, each with guns operated by four-man teams. During the battle of the Somme these were used as a back-stop against breakthroughs. A French report of 1917 refers to an original organization of three companies per battalion, this being increased to 'four companies of from 150 to 170 men each, supplied with 30 automatic rifles to a company, or 120 to a battalion' (US War Department 1917a: 18). The Madsen, with its 25-round top-mounted box magazine, was effective enough, but its early deployment does not appear to have been calculated for maximum impact. Moreover, it was concluded, rightly or wrongly, that being made in Denmark meant that the weapon could not be reproduced, and that it 'could never replace a machine gun' (Cron 2001: 120). Nevertheless, the Madsen continued to see limited German use after 1916.

The Parabellum machine gun also had a history stretching back before the war, being the result of a DWM commercial project for a light weapon with a modified Maxim mechanism that came to fruition in 1913, but

which did not immediately interest the German Government. When adopted, it would be in two different models: the first, which retained a water-filled jacket, was referred to as the MG 14; and the second, which was air cooled, the LMG 14. With limited production, and because it was configured essentially for aerial use, the Parabellum failed to make the grade as an infantry weapon, but was used on aircraft and Zeppelin airships.

The Bergmann company of Gaggenau, Baden, with its designer Louis Schmeisser, developed a prototype belt-fed, water-cooled machine gun as early as 1901. This was improved through several models, including a new type in 1910 which could take not only canvas belts but 'Ruszitska' disintegrating metallic-link belts of an Austrian design. Nevertheless, Bergmann machine guns failed to find a significant market until 1915, when the hunt for light machine guns led Bergmann to modify its weapon radically by removing the water jacket and replacing its twin grips with a short stock. This first Bergmann LMG 15 fired from an open bolt, but was soon superseded by an LMG 15nA model – the 'nA' standing for *neuer Art* or 'new type' – firing from a closed bolt. Though not universal issue, the Bergmann LMG was successful enough to see service, on aircraft, as well as about 5,000 being manufactured for the infantry. Its practicality for mobile ground use was enhanced by a bracket to take a belt box, and the fitting of a bipod and carry handle. It had a cyclic rate of 500rds/min, and its main battlefield use was as a stopgap in late 1916 and 1917, quite a number being used on the Eastern Front. French reports were uncomplimentary, mentioning a battlefield organization of three-gun groups, each gun firing 30 rounds in turn, to avoid overheating. That the Bergmann was dismissed as a candidate for general issue

Abteilung A of the armourers' course at Halberstadt under Instructor Bock, 19 February–26 March 1918. Bock is almost certainly pictured centre front, an officer decorated with both grades of the Iron Cross. His pupils include men from various branches including the infantry and mountain troops. The machine guns shown include not only the MG 08 and Russian Maxim (right), but the Bergmann MG 15nA and the French Chauchat light machine gun (foreground). On the left are the British Vickers (with fluted barrel jacket), the French Hotchkiss and the German Dreyse. A rangefinder is shown on the right.

THE MG 08/15 EXPOSED

7.92×57mm Maschinengewehr 08/15

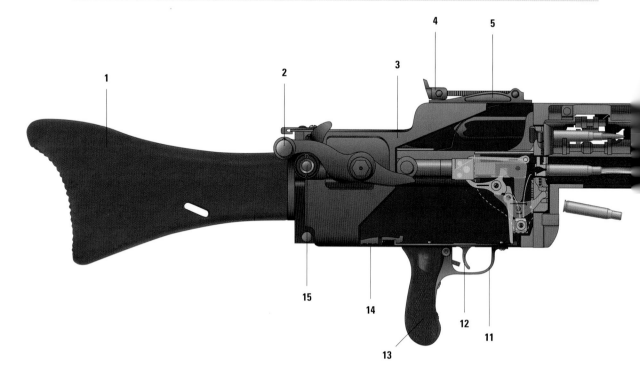

1. *Schulterstütze* (buttstock)
2. *Schloßhebel* (lock lever / crank handle)
3. *Kastendeckel* (receiver cover)
4. *Visier* (sight)
5. *Visierfuß* (sight base)
6. *Gewehrkupplungsstück* (coupling piece for steam tube)
7. *Laufmantel* (barrel jacket)
8. *Korn* (sight bead, offset to left)
9. *Rückstoßverstarker* (muzzle booster)
10. *Zweibein* (bipod)
11. *Abzugsbügel* (trigger guard)
12. *Abzug* (trigger)
13. *Griff* (grip)
14. *Kastenboden* (receiver base)
15. *Sperrklinke* (pawl)
16. *Schloß* (lock)
17. *Gurthebelachse* (belt lever axis)
18. *Patronenträger* (cartridge carrier)
19. *Zuführer* (feed)
20. *Gurtschieber* (belt pusher)
21. *Kugel* (bullet)
22. *Hülse* (empty cartridge)
23. *Schlagbolzen* (firing pin)
24. *Rechter Patronenträgerhebel* (right cartridge carrier lever)
25. *Abzugshebel* (sear)
26. *Sicherungssperrklinke* (safety catch)
27. *Federstift* (spring bar)

After the slow start at Spandau, MG 08/15 output increased dramatically during 1917, with six other firms joining production. Industrial efforts now focused specifically on machine guns, artillery and their projectiles, under the 'Hindenburg Programme'. By the end of the war the MG 08/15 was easily the most numerous of German machine guns, with a total of about 130,000 made. (To put this into context, some 72,000 MG 08s were made, 50,000 at DWM and the remainder at Spandau.) By far the largest number produced was in 1918.

MG 08/15 production

Spandau Government Arsenal	50,000		
Erfurt Government Arsenal	33,000	Rheinische Metallwaaren- und Maschinenfabrik	7,000
Maschinenfabrik Augsburg-Nürnberg (MAN)	14,000	Deutsche Waffen- und Munitionsfabriken (DWM)	2,000
Siemens & Halske	13,000	*Total*	130,000
J.P. Sauer und Sohn, Suhl	11,000	(Goldsmith 1989: 169)	

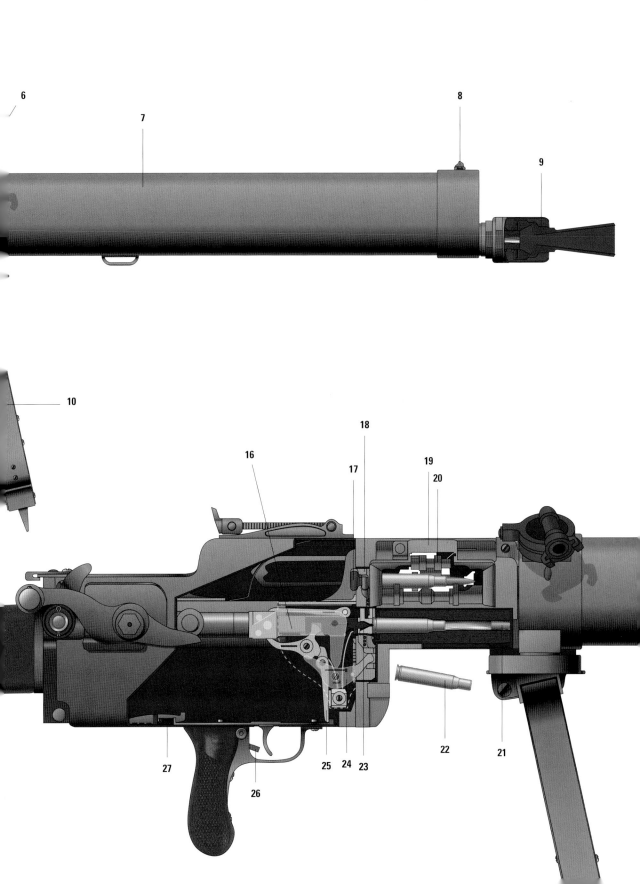

Landsturm infantry with the Bergmann LMG 15nA. The short-recoil Bergmann weighed 12.9kg and fired from metal link belts. It was a useful stopgap, but as an ad hoc conversion from a water-cooled system to air cooling it was susceptible to overheating. The main use of this weapon was on the Eastern Front.

throughout the infantry would seem to suggest that some of the criticism was justified.

The old Dreyse works of Sömerda in Thuringia made its name with the famous 'Needle Gun' that equipped Prussian armies in the wars of 1866 and 1870–71. Early in the new century, and again with the involvement of Louis Schmeisser, the company began to design machine guns with a pivoting lock action. By 1912 the Dreyse catalogue featured a water-cooled, belt-fed, recoil-operated weapon; some were used by the German Army in Palestine, and others supplied to Bulgaria. After the outbreak of war the Dreyse was also considered as a multi-use weapon, and fitted with a bracket that allowed it to be used in conjunction with a bipod. Despite some infantry use in the 'light' role, retention of water cooling and a complex mechanism ensured that it never became a standard-issue light machine gun.

While all these weapons did duty, Merkatz and the Gewehrprüfungskommission continued to pursue the objective of a 'universal' machine gun. Items developed as part of the programme included a new machine-gun lock, similar to that of the Vickers, and a tripod with telescoping front legs. The apogee of these efforts was the MG 16, a relatively light water-cooled gun, based on the Maxim design, with just a single spade grip and trigger. A very few MG 16s were produced at Erfurt; but by now a lightened version of the MG 08 had also been produced, the result of which was that the idea of disrupting manufacture of a weapon that was tried and tested was abandoned, and the lightened MG 08 took pride of place almost by default.

The new light machine gun was standardized before the end of 1915, and despite the fact that perhaps only a couple of thousand had been produced by 1916, the official designation MG 08/15 stuck. Its rationale was brutally simple: take an MG 08, and leave the recoiling parts of the gun mechanism, including the lock, untouched; cut weight from everything else to create a Maxim that was portable by one man, and could be fired from a shoulder stock with a conventional trigger. Getting to this point and putting the MG 08/15 into mass production was not as simple as this sounds, however, and involved many individual changes. The most obvious were replacement of the sled with a small bipod, and the fitting of a wooden stock and pistol grip. Less apparent but equally significant were reduction of the water jacket to a slimmer profile with a 3- rather than 4-litre capacity, and the shaving of many components to reduce the amount of metal. These trimmings included altering the shape of the receiver and reducing the thickness of its walls to eliminate dead space, and also the omission of the ejection tube. The optical sight bracket was deleted. Other changes improved

the practicality of the new gun in its new role. The rear sight was changed, and the new trigger acquired a safety blocking its movement when applied. A bracket allowed for a belt drum, and a carry sling was fitted. These slings were made of various materials, some from the latter part of World War I being of an *Ersatz* composition of plaited paper.

Frustration with slow progress, and the heaviness of the 'light' gun, extended right to the top. As Germany's senior soldier, Generalfeldmarschall Paul von Hindenburg, put it:

> The infantry was supplied with a light machine gun, which might have been lighter and more simple, for it required too many men. It was necessary to come to a decision, however, for preparations for manufacture had to be made, and these took months and months. Each company of infantry was to have four and later six, of these light guns. (Quoted in Cron 2001: 113)

Despite the slow start to production, the MG 08/15 was undoubtedly a practical machine gun, lighter than the MG 08, allowing the German Army to counter enemy weapons, and to employ new and more imaginative infantry tactics. Nevertheless, the MG 08/15 was still weighty, being 19.5kg with full water jacket but without ammunition. This compared to 15.2kg for a loaded Lewis gun, or just 9.5kg for a loaded Chauchat.

Interestingly, as well as producing 50,000 MG 08/15s, Spandau also produced 23,000 examples of an LMG 08/15. This was a version of the 08/15 for aircraft use, further lightened by dispensing with water cooling and cutting slots through the barrel jacket. It built on experience gained with the LMG 08, a Fokker conversion of the MG 08 to air cooling created for aircraft in 1915. The reasons both these weapons worked effectively enough in the air, when such a conversion would not have fared well on the ground, were essentially twofold. The first was that in air combat, ammunition was limited and bursts tended to be of short duration as aircraft passed each other, or overflew ground targets. The second was that the slipstream while in flight cooled the armament. In either event, the opportunity for overheating was limited.

Near the end of the war Erfurt produced an air-cooled MG 08/18, again based on the MG 08/15. This used a barrel with a slim perforated jacket and weighed about 15kg. The MG 08/18 was issued to mountain and bicycle units before the Armistice, and was a significant weapon during the interwar period. Perhaps predictably, however, it was prone to overheating, not helped by the difficulty of performing barrel changes.

USE

German Maxims at war

MACHINE-GUN ISSUE IN 1914

Much was achieved in the run-up to war, but issue and an even distribution of the MG 08 was still incomplete. So it was that in August 1914, the four-battalion Reserve-Infanterie-Regiment Nr. 130, the Lehr-Infanterie-Regiment and Reserve-Infanterie-Regimenter Nrs 1, 3 and 18 all had two machine-gun companies. Conversely, quite a few other *Reserve-Infanterie-Regimenter* had yet to form their first *Maschinengewehr-Kompagnie*. The total numbers of machine-gun companies were: 219 with the infantry regiments; 16 with the *Jäger-Bataillone*; and 88 with the *Reserve-Infanterie-Regimenter*. Additionally, 43 'machine-gun detachments' were ready for the *Ersatz* ('supplementary') divisions: 15 detachments allotted to fortresses; 11 with the cavalry; five in reserve; and a few others apparently scattered in garrison towns. The practical result was that Reserve and Landwehr formations went under-equipped for some time: during the Battle of the Marne in September 1914, for example, quite a few divisions lacked the full paper complement of 24 guns. One division had only six.

Exactly how many machine guns the German Army had at the outbreak of war has been argued over ever since. The Entente Powers miscounted and often exaggerated, and German commentators, particularly after 1918, minimized the number. Clarification has been found in a set of figures compiled for the German authorities on 3 August 1914, originally produced with a view to determining how many weapons still lacked shields. In order to do this, the number of weapons in service with the Army was calculated. The count showed 4,411 MG 08s, 398 MG 01s and 18 MG 99s. (Interestingly, two MG 09s were also found, these being the Maxim 'Commercial' model gun, with a Vickers-type lock, mounted on a tripod made by DWM for export.) This total of 4,829 guns correlates approximately with the serial numbers observed on DWM and Spandau weapons dated from 1908 to 1914. Moreover, the data also confirms that while the field army was now essentially equipped with the MG 08, the remaining MG 01 and MG 99 types supplemented MG 08s in fortresses, fixed positions and reserves. The guns in garrisons and fortresses were not always allotted in identically sized units. So it was that while the 15 fortress detachments accounted for 150 guns, each forming a detachment of ten, the western town of Metz contained no fewer than 133 MG 08 and 80 MG 01 weapons. Together with 28 MG 08s, the two MG 09s were at the Prussian town of Graudenz on the eastern frontier. With only trivial exceptions, guns in fortresses and other defensive positions and depots were deployed in even-numbered groups, suggesting a generalized use of two-gun 'platoons'.

OPERATING THE MG 08

The MG 08 Döberitz course handbook (Tilly 1915) begins with a description of the weapon, and stresses the need for gunners to study and become practised in its operation. No fewer than 22 pages are devoted to explaining the working parts of the MG 08, the lock alone being regarded as made up of 16 different components. All this is conveyed without the aid of any pictorial reference within the pamphlet, suggesting that students were standing by a gun during instruction. Treatment of the gun during operation occupied a relatively modest five pages, and was divided into three parts: preparation; firing; and post-firing actions.

Machine-gunners of Königlich Sächsisches 4. Infanterie-Regiment Nr. 103 with MG 08 and sled mount in the depressed position for prone firing. The gun is equipped with an optical sight, and the man to the right has the cylindrical water can. The ammunition boxes are the large, 500-round Modell 1911, each of which contains two 250-round belts, one either side of a central divider.

Preparing to fire

Under preparation were covered such points as checking that the barrel jacket was filled with water, the weapon was seated in its trunnions, the steam tube was connected, and that all necessary spares and ammunition were to hand. Once the gun commander completed his checks he reported to the platoon commander, as for example on the condition of the gun, and the numbers of belts and rounds to hand.

The basic loading and firing sequence was common to all the variants of the German Maxim gun, and could be commenced with the gun's top cover closed or open. (Under combat conditions the cover was generally left closed to exclude dirt.) First, a full belt of ammunition was fed into the feed block from the right, and the metal tab pulled out to the left until the belt was caught and held by the pawls. Then the crank handle was rotated and held in the forward position, while the belt was pulled across the feedway, and slightly forward, with the left hand. The crank was then allowed to spring back, the mechanism gripping the first round. Pushing the crank forward, and again pulling the belt and letting the crank spring back completed the process and the gun was ready to fire in full-automatic mode. Interestingly, it was also possible to operate the gun one shot at a time by not pulling the belt a second time, then pushing forward and releasing the crank between each shot. Given a handy supply of belted ammunition, loading Maxim types took only a few seconds – much faster indeed to do than to describe.

Filling belts was a laborious operation often done by the machine-gun troops themselves, preferably well in advance of action, as

Machine-gunners in fatigue uniform with a stripped-down MG 08. Among the parts removed are the barrel (back left), the grip assembly (back right), the lock (centre left) and the feed block (front left).

ammunition was commonly supplied as loose rounds in boxes. A German patent for a Maxim gun belt-loading machine was filed as early as January 1896 by Hugo Borchardt, and the Borchardt patent number '91227' is seen on some examples. By World War I there was more than one model of filler, though they operated on similar principles. The Gürtfuller 16, issued one with each gun from 1916, came in its own *Kasten* or wooden box. Its major components were a gear system with a revolving cylinder, handle, small hopper at the top, and a clamp at the bottom, by means of which the unit could be firmly attached to a work bench or table The operator engaged an empty belt over the cylinder of the mechanism and filled the hopper with rounds, noses pointing away from himself. Pushing in and turning the bar of the handle clockwise about 25 degrees thrust a single round into the belt. Returning the handle and repeating the operation lined up the next hole in the belt and thrust in the next round; and so it continued, recharging the hopper and working the handle until all 250 spaces were full. Other items supplied with the Gürtfuller 16 included a mounting bracket, a spare gear, a gauge to check cartridge seating, a device to open stiff belt pockets and an attachment for belt unloading. Belt fillers were easier to fabricate than machine guns and perhaps for this reason were made by quite a few manufacturers. DWM, Berlin and the Fortuna Werk at Cannstadt on the outskirts of Stuttgart appear to have made the greatest number, but they were also supplied by Herman Gradewitz and Schulze, both of Berlin; Roth & Müller, Stuttgart; Pfister of Oberschöneweide; Union of Bochum; Friedrich Keese; and probably others.

The V. Armeekorps assistant armourers' course at Posen, 1918. In the centre is an MG 08, and to the left an MG 08/15. The piece to the right is also an MG 08, but sectioned for instructional purposes.

Firing

The MG 08 was fired by holding the walnut-wood spade grips, pushing with the thumb to disengage the safety, and depressing the trigger bar. Flame and bullets erupted from the muzzle, the degree of drama in the display depending on the presence or absence of a 'flash hider', and whether it was night. A stream of hot empty brass cases showered from the ejection tube at the lower front of the receiver. The beating heart of the gun was its toggle lock and a balanced arrangement of springs and levers harnessing the recoil of each cartridge as it fired. Upon firing, the barrel and lock recoiled together a short distance before the toggle lock broke open, by which time the bullet had left the barrel and pressure had begun to drop off. With backward momentum decreasing, it no longer overcame the power of the fusee spring, which now pulled the lock back into battery. Simultaneously, the lock gripped two cartridges in the course of its movement, namely the one in the chamber and a fresh one from the belt, which itself was advanced through the feed by the movement of the barrel. Provided the mechanism had been pre-primed with two rounds and the belt correctly positioned, the weapon continued to cycle, banging away at an average rate of 450rds/min until the ammunition was exhausted a little over 30 seconds later. More usually, however, the weapon was operated in bursts interspersed with longer or shorter pauses, according to the urgency of the fire mission, the needs of observation, aim correction and ammunition conservation. MG 08 manuals show the gunner's forefingers hooked over the top bar of the grips, to give better control, as with the British Vickers.

Though some commentators have described the rate of fire of the MG 08 as 'sedate', and to modern ears its tone is a loud steady 'chugging' – a distinctive, hollow, slow 'tac-tac-tac' compared to the Vickers' faster 'rat-tat-tat' – in 1914 its cyclic rate was comparable to that of its contemporaries. Moreover, for targets such as charging horses, or men struggling over shell-pocked ground, up to seven or eight rounds a second could seem like a wall of fire. The Maxim system was neat compared to that of many other weapons, and by standards of the time remarkable. In a fraction of a second following each detonation of a cartridge the bullet fired, the mechanism unlocked, the empty cartridge was extracted and ejected, the mechanism re-cocked, the feed advanced, a new round was chambered and the mechanism locked again.

While the gunner aimed and fired – at the behest of a gun commander or of his own volition – and could work alone if required, it was quicker and helped avoid stoppages if a loader was stationed close to his right. The loader positioned the belt box and offered up the tab, making sure the belt snaked smoothly from the container through the feed. This was vital because the belt could set up a wave motion, eventually twisting and jamming the gun. Belts were packed ready, loosely folded in a 'Z' shape, layer on layer, so they worked into the mechanism from the container at even tension, without snagging, pulling or stretching. Standard World War I German belts had a small spacer bar every third round. These spacers helped prevent rounds being jostled out of position in the box and assisted alignment through the feed. If the gun had to be moved

significantly to a new arc of fire, the assistant not only helped the gunner but repositioned the belt box square to the breech. While the gunner needed to sight the weapon over the barrel, the loader had more freedom to conceal himself, especially if a gun commander provided observation. Careful loaders remained below parapets or prone, so long as an efficient ammunition feed was ensured.

Devastating as it often was, the MG 08 could not be described as either effortless to use, or particularly ergonomic. As Otto Lais reported of the stamina and concentration required of sustained action on the Somme:

An MG 08 with *Rückstoßverstärker* captured by 11th (Service) Battalion (Accrington), The East Lancashire Regiment, in the latter part of World War I. The battalion captured 17 machine guns during the clearance of Ploegsteert Wood in September 1918. (Lancashire Infantry Museum Collection; author's photograph)

> Speak loudly, slowly and clearly to yourself; "Forward – feed – back [with the cocking lever] then the same again! Safety catch to the right! Press down, tak-tak tak-tak, once more rapid fire slams into the clay pit in front of us! Tall columns of steam rise from almost all of the machine guns. The steam hoses of most of the guns have been torn off or shot away. Skin hangs in ribbons from the fingers of the gunners and the gun commanders' hands are burned. The left thumb became a swollen, shapeless lump of flesh from the constant pressure on the safety catch. The hands felt like they were cramped from the slight vibrations of the grips of the gun. 18,000 rounds! The other gun in the platoon had a jam. Schütze Schw. falls from a shot to the head and falls over the belt he was feeding. The belt twists, causing the cartridges to enter the feed opening at an angle and become jammed. The next Schützen forward. The dead man is laid to one side. The gunner takes the feeder out, removes the rounds and reloads. Firing, nothing but firing, barrel changes, fetching ammunition, laying the dead and wounded down in the cratered ground. (Quoted in Sheldon 2005: 142–43)

Maintaining fire

Over and above combat fire, the team had to be well versed in maintenance and stoppages. Indeed, the standard machine-gun course lasted a month, and of this the majority of time was devoted to the mechanism and care of the gun and the diagnosis and rectification of stoppages and faults. Even when the weapon functioned perfectly, it required barrel changes and refilling with water. A spare barrel was fitted on the sled mount of the MG 08, and regulation dictated that a change be executed every 5,000 rounds. Additional barrels for the MG 08, or the MG 08/15, were carried in leather cases with shoulder slings. The speed with which the water in the barrel jacket boiled depended on the rate of fire, but sooner or later it did boil, and – turning to steam – travelled down the flexible hose to the condenser can. With the steam becoming liquid again, it was now possible to tip the water back into the barrel, but inevitably, and even without serious leaks, some vapour would be lost, giving rise to a need for additional water supply. Usually this was satisfied by starting with some water in the can, and keeping additional containers on the fire position. However, desperate circumstances led to desperate measures, as was reported by Otto Lais:

> The cooling water turns to seething steam with continuous firing. In the heat of battle, the steam overflow pipe slips out of its fixing on the water jacket. With a great hiss a jet of steam goes up, providing a superb target for the enemy. It is the greatest good fortune they have the sun in their eyes and we have it at our backs. The enemy closes up nearer. We fire on endlessly. There is less steam. A further barrel change is urgent. The cooling water has almost steamed away. 'Where's the water?' bawls the gunner. 'Get the mineral water out of the dugout!', 'There's none left Unteroffizier!'... We have got to fire. A gunner rushes into the crater with the water container and urinates into it. A second pisses into it too – quick refill! The British have closed to grenade throwing range and hand grenades fly backwards and forwards. The barrel change is complete, the water jacket refilled. (Quoted in Sheldon 2005: 142)

During pauses in fire the team were instructed to top up the coolant, lubricate as required or clean away any fouling caused by powder (Tilly 1915). No. 4 and No. 5 looked to ammunition supply, also retrieving and packing empty belts back into ammunition boxes, supported by any reserve gunners. Any gun part not quickly made serviceable by the team was handed back for the immediate attention of the *Waffenmeister-Unteroffizier* (armourer NCO).

Even when the machine gun was efficiently oiled, watered and fed with ammunition, weapon stoppages could occur, and in diagnosing the cause, skilled gunners observed the position of the cocking lever. Commonly, it stopped in one of four positions when fire was interrupted (see overleaf). The skill of the crew in identifying and rectifying failures under pressure, and perhaps under fire, was key to the efficiency of the machine-gun unit. Where weapons were deployed in two-gun 'platoons' or singly it might

Bild 40.

Das Festhalten des M.G. und des Schlosses mit Patronen.

Beim Herausnehmen des Schlosses aus dem M.G. mit Patronen den Zeigefinger
zwischen Patronenträger und die Verstärkung des Schloßgehäuses legen.

Unloading or clearing a stoppage by lifting the breech cover and removing the lock complete with cartridges. The index finger is placed between the cartridge carrier and the reinforcement of the lock housing. The independent machine-gun detachments wore *Jäger*-style shakos. From Merkatz 1917 & 1918.

even spell success or failure for the holding or taking of a position. Where simple steps such as working the crank, freeing belts or broken cartridges, cleaning, lubrication or adjustment of a fusee spring failed to get the gun going, it might be necessary to change the lock, or other parts. The kit with which to do the job was stowed on the MG 08 sled, and in separate tool kits. Among the items usually kept on the sled were: a pair of spare locks and cartridge extractors, in small boxes one either side toward the front; cleaning patches and a muzzle gland, in an even smaller box, back left; a spare barrel, along the right-hand side; two boxes containing lubricant, rear centre; and – clipped in holders about the centre – hand tools. These last were tongs, and a chamber-cleaning stick. A flat multi-purpose spanner was also often carried.

As there were other things that could go awry – and many MG 08s were used on improvised mounts, while the 08/15 was usually fitted with a shoulder stock – separate tool kits were also carried into the front line. The standard MG 08 section tool chest was a clever adaptation of the 500-round Modell 1911 machine-gun ammunition box, fitted with a tray. Its contents included: hammers and spanners; screwdrivers; pliers; lock-assembly punch; oil can; dummy cartridges; spare recoil spring; and even a small wooden anvil. If more work was required than could be immediately achieved by the gunners, weapons needed the attention of the company *Waffenmeister-Unteroffizier* and his supply box. This large wooden chest was a converted MG 08 transport chest with trays inserted, and the company armourers also attended to the small arms of the unit.

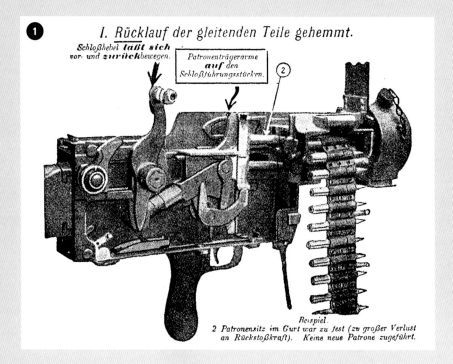

1 *I. Rücklauf der gleitenden Teile gehemmt.*

Schloßhebel läßt sich vor- und zurückbewegen.

Patronenträgerarme auf den Schloßführungsstücken.

2

Beispiel.
2 Patronensitz im Gurt war zu fest (zu großer Verlust an Rückstoßkraft). Keine neue Patrone zugeführt.

Common stoppages, illustrated by the MG 08/15

(**1**) Lock lever capable of forward and rearward motion, but recoil of moving parts obstructed. May be due to: cartridges too tight in belt; worn barrel; over-tensioned recoil spring.

(**2**) Lock lever unable to move rearward: forward movement of working parts jammed. Possible causes of stoppage include: belt stuck in feeder, or twisted; damaged cartridge; cartridges too far to rear in belt.

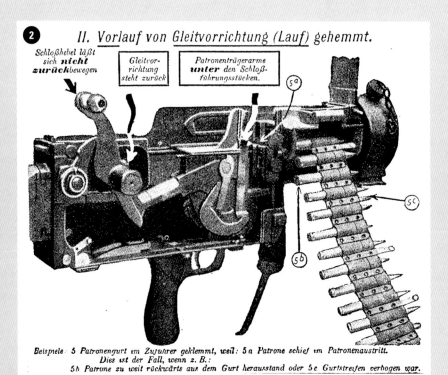

2 *II. Vorlauf von Gleitvorrichtung (Lauf) gehemmt.*

Schloßhebel läßt sich nicht zurückbewegen.

Gleitvorrichtung steht zurück.

Patronenträgerarme unter den Schloßführungsstücken.

5a

5c

5b

Beispiele. 5 Patronengurt im Zuführer geklemmt, weil: 5a Patrone schief im Patronenaustritt.
Dies ist der Fall, wenn z. B.:
5b Patrone zu weit rückwärts aus dem Gurt herausstand oder 5c Gurtstreifen verbogen war.

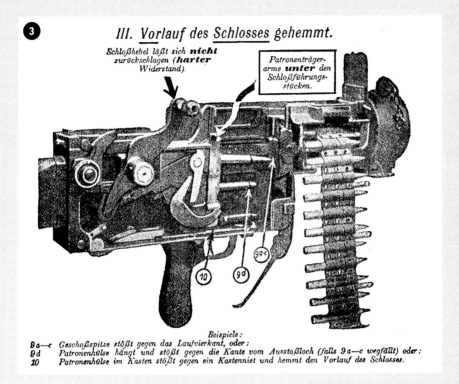

III. Vorlauf des Schlosses gehemmt.

*Schloßhebel läßt sich **nicht** zurückschlagen (**harter** Widerstand).*

*Patronenträgerarme **unter** den Schloßführungsstücken.*

Beispiele:

9 a—c *Geschoßspitze stößt gegen das Laufvierkant, oder:*
9 d *Patronenhülse hängt und stößt gegen die Kante vom Ausstoßloch (falls 9 a—c wegfällt) oder:*
10 *Patronenhülse im Kasten stößt gegen ein Kastenniet und hemmt den Vorlauf des Schlosses.*

(**3**) Lock lever stuck in forward position, advance of lock obstructed. Causes may include: bullet point jammed against chamber; cartridge stuck against ejection hole or rivet in receiver.

(**4**) Lock lever back close to pawl, rearmost breech motion hindered and cartridge carrier not returned to position. Causes may include: under-tensioned recoil spring; damaged or poorly loaded belt.

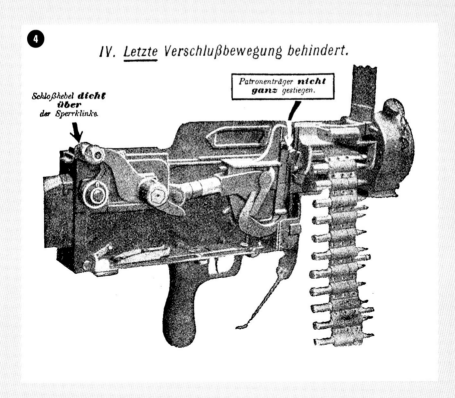

IV. Letzte Verschlußbewegung behindert.

*Schloßhebel **dicht über** der Sperrklinke.*

*Patronenträger **nicht ganz** gestiegen.*

Post-firing actions

With cessation of fire the optical sight was dismounted and put back into its case, the gun unloaded and the ejection port cleared, loose rounds being returned to belts. Any spare parts used by gun crews were now replenished from the armourer's chest and everything else cleaned and put away.

The surest way to unload a Maxim was to keep shooting until both the belt was expended and the last rounds remaining in the mechanism were fired. When this was not possible, things became more complicated. The next quickest method was to work the crank handle forwards and release it twice. This allowed one unspent round to fall out while another was left in the ejection tube. The belt could now be disengaged from the feed block by pushing on it while holding the pawl latch. This method did not allow the gunner to check the mechanism, however, and now left a couple of live rounds to be located and retrieved. A common field method was removal of three rounds from the belt near the feed block, then firing until empty. Given time and opportunity, the gun could also be unloaded by unlatching and opening the top cover, pushing forward the crank and holding it there. With the extractor in the down position, and the firing pin unable to reach the live cartridge on the face of the extractor, the gunner gripped the lock between thumb and forefinger. Keeping the forefinger across the front of the lock body so that the extractor could not be raised, he now lifted the lock bodily out of the breech. The last round or two were removed from the lock, the soldier gripping them just above the base of the cartridge. This could not be accomplished quickly with a hot gun, however. In any event, crews were well advised to check any Maxim carefully before moving or handling it as it was possible to leave rounds in the mechanism, even without the presence of a belt.

An early-war photograph from the Eastern Front campaign showing that at least *in extremis* the complete MG 08 equipment could be carried by just one man. As weapon and sled mount together weighed upwards of 53kg, this was very much an emergency or short-distance option for a strong individual.

LEFT and BELOW Details of a 1918 Erfurt-manufactured MG 08/15, showing the *Trommel* or 'drum' magazine. This particular weapon was captured by 2/5th Battalion, The Loyal North Lancashire Regiment, commanded by Lieutenant-Colonel C.F. Hitchins. The MG 08/15's equivalent to the MG 08's section tool chest was a leather tool roll, issued one with each weapon. This contained some similar items, and also a lock and muzzle gland.

OPERATING THE MG 08/15

Preparing to fire

The gunner held the pistol grip with the buttstock into his shoulder, initially with the finger clear of the trigger, and pushed off the safety. Then, preferably with the left arm bracing the butt of the gun, he squeezed the trigger. While the accuracy of the MG 08 depended much upon having a correctly set up and tightened mounting, the MG 08/15 gunner assumed greater responsibility for effect by way of his body

39

position and steadiness. Ideally, the weapon was fired prone, perhaps from a depression allowing maximum use of cover, with both legs of the bipod not only squarely on the ground, but with the small prongs at the ends of the legs slightly penetrating the ground surface. The firer could further steady himself by keeping his shoulders roughly square to the target, his body mass behind the breech, and slightly opening his legs, with or without bent knee. Where such textbook posture was impossible due to ground or battle conditions, the barrel jacket was best rested on a steady firm surface, as for example sandbags which had the added advantage of a degree of 'give' to create a groove to cradle and support the gun.

Firing and reloading

Like the MG 08, the MG 08/15 could be fed from a belt box with a second crewman acting as loader, but this weapon also took a drum, or *Trommel*, magazine, namely the Patronenkasten 16. Each steel drum magazine was designed to house a 100-round belt, and they were supplied in pairs packed in a wooden box, though they could also be left attached to the belt-box bracket on the right-hand side of the MG 08/15. To charge the drum, the top flipped open and the belt was wound onto a spool, the tab stowed neatly into the bracket slot, and the crank lever locked. For firing, the crank lever was raised to unlock the belt, the tab freed, the drum slid onto the bracket, and the belt fed into the feed block in the usual way. A reminder to 'lift crank to fire' was stamped into the drum, with the wording 'Feuer – Kurbel Hoch'. Though the 100-round drum was less suitable than 250-round belts for sustained fire, the lack of a trailing belt offered some advantages in terms of mobility and rapidity of deployment.

MG 08/15 firing positions (opposite)

(**1**) Infantryman in basic prone fire position, 1917. The gunner lies squarely behind the weapon, legs slightly apart, right hand on the pistol grip, left hand braced across the butt. The gun is steadied, and the target presented minimized from the front. For fire around cover it was also possible to turn both legs to one side.

(**2**) Infantryman firing from shell hole, summer 1918. Left arm braced on butt, elbows rested and body steadied against lip of crater. For sustained fire the hose would require a water can.

(**3**) 'Assault Fire' position using a belt drum, for automatic fire during an advance. Owing to inherent inaccuracy this posture was most useful as a 'suppressive' measure. Though 'Assault Fire' was used during World War I, this image is based on one shown in Reichskriegsministerium 1931. Note the 'blank firing' attachment on the MG 08/15 muzzle.

(**4**) Firing over a valley from a forward slope during training, with gunner in fatigue uniform, *c.*1939. This difficult 'back' position was best used only in emergencies, and then very briefly, due to the stress imposed on the gunner's leg. Nevertheless, it also featured in official manuals.

Machine-gun training

Writing in 1917, Longstaff and Atteridge described the training of the German machine-gun company as follows:

The Regulations note that besides the six guns attached to the machine-gun detachment, it has in time of peace two older guns, which are used for instruction, so as to minimise the wear and tear of the service pieces. Elaborate instructions are given as to how all the material of the battery is to be kept in good order.

The Regulations for the preliminary drills include exercises in taking cover and handling the machine gun in various positions — standing behind a parapet, kneeling, seated, and lying-down. The first firing exercises are with blank cartridges. Two kinds of firing are distinguished – continuous firing, and salvo, or volley-firing, this latter being a discharge of fifty cartridges, usually employed for range-finding purposes.

Continuous firing is again divided into three varieties:

(1) Fire concentrated on a single point,

(2) firing with a horizontal sweeping movement, and

(3) firing with continual change of elevation, so as to give depth to the beaten zone on which the bullets fall.

After the preliminary drills the detachment is exercised in target practice on the range and field firing. It is directed that in all practices care is to be taken that the same men fire the same gun, so as to become familiar with any peculiarity in its shooting. There is a direction which one expects in case of artillery practice, but which seems hardly needed with machine guns. At all firing practices, one of the non-commissioned officers is responsible for having a supply of cotton ready to be put in the ears of those working the guns. The range practices include firing at targets up to 1,500 yards [1,370m], with slow or rapid fire, concentrated and sweeping fire, fire with varying elevation, and with the machine gunner kneeling, seated, or lying down. Elaborate instructions are given and there are special tests for second and first class shots, and those who pass these tests qualify by an additional test as pointers.

The field-firing practices are divided into firing with a single machine gun, firing with the section of two guns, and firing with the whole battery of six guns. It is directed that these practices shall take place on at least twelve different days and at various seasons of the year. Everything is to be carried out as far as possible under battle conditions. Great stress is laid on the choice of targets, and of the moment for coming into action, and it is noted that the heavy expenditure of ammunition and the wear and tear of the material restrict the time during which the guns can be kept firing, and therefore make it all-important that the fire should be efficacious. Oblique or flank fire is the most effective against troops of all kinds, and the only kind of fire that will give much result against artillery with shields on the guns. As it may be difficult to pass orders by word of mouth amid the noise of battle, officers and men are to be practised in giving and obeying orders by signal.

The inspection of a machine-gun company or detachment is not to be confined to mere parade movements, but is to

An *Offizier-Stellvertreter* or 'deputy' officer on the ranges, *c*.1917. With the MG 08 sled depressed, the firer's elbows rest on pads on the rear legs of the mount. This gun is fitted with the *Mantelpanzer* or 'armoured jacket' over the barrel assembly, water-jacket front shield and *Unterschild* ('under shield'), fitted inside the front of the mounting.

include actual firing. Arrangements are also made from time to time for experimental firing under the direction of the General Staff, in order to obtain data for the solution of questions that it is studying. Prizes are given by the Government for … special competitions in shooting with the machine gun at the end of the annual course. For instance, the best shots among the non-commissioned officers at any military station are allowed to compete in target practice, in which each fires 250 shots; the prize is a watch given in the name of the Kaiser, and engraved with the name of the winner. The usual machine-gun targets are bands of canvas, or cardboard, representing the heads and shoulders of lines of skirmishers. These are placed either at right angles or obliquely to the line of fire, or several targets are arranged behind each other to represent successive lines of skirmishers.

There is a liberal allowance of cartridges; each company or detachment is annually allotted 110,000 ball cartridges and 100,000 blank cartridges, fitted with a dummy bullet of soft wood, or compressed paper, so as to produce sufficient recoil to work the breech mechanism. It is laid down that 70,000 ball cartridges are to be expended in the field firing, and 7,500 at the annual inspection. It is forbidden to economise in any way the 70,000 cartridges allotted to the field firing. If by any chance it is not possible to use them all in a given year, the unexpended cartridges are to be carried forward to the following year and added to those used at the field firing. The 100,000 blank cartridges are to be used thus: 40,000 for drill and training purposes, and the remaining 60,000 at the annual manoeuvres.

Each soldier of the machine-gun company or detachment has a book, in which a record is kept of his shooting at every practice in which he takes part. The commander of the company has thus a permanent record showing the relative efficiency of all his men. When a company or detachment receives a new gun, its shooting is carefully tested on the range, 1,000 cartridges being allowed for this purpose. A diagram of the shooting is made, and this is kept as a guide in the subsequent use of the gun. (Longstaff & Atteridge 1917: 155–56)

An MG 08/15 team on the machine-gun course at Hammelburg, 1918. The hose from the water jacket leads to the small box-type condenser can. The can was about the same dimensions as a 250-round belt box, and equipped with a swivel spout which allowed water collected to be poured back into the barrel jacket. The camp at Hammelburg opened in 1895 as a range for the Bavarian Army, the machine-gun school there being established at the end of 1914.

TACTICAL PRINCIPLES

According to the *Felddienst-Ordnung* ('Field Service Regulations') of 1908, the effect of machine guns depended on the correct setting of sights, possibility of observation, and density of the target. This would be further influenced by surprise, the number of guns and the strength of enemy fire. Maximum effectiveness required concentration of fire from multiple weapons, preferably from a flank. In practice, the tactical effectiveness of the individual MG 08 depended to a great degree on how it was set up. The steady if bulky sled mount was relatively difficult to conceal, but matters were much improved by having more than one possible firing point, and height adjusted to match both terrain and cover. If these factors were managed correctly, the chances of taking the enemy by surprise, and preferably in enfilade, were vastly increased. Enfilade fire was particularly advantageous as shooting from the side of the unit increased its apparent depth and density.

To change the height of the sled mount, spring-loaded handles on the front legs of the mount were squeezed to free them and allow their angle to be altered, so raising or lowering the barrel in relation to the ground. In flatter or more open terrain, the mount and crew were best kept as low as possible. When firing over undulating ground, or through an aperture, a higher setting for the sled might be required with the gun team seated or kneeling. One variation adopted within a trench or shell hole was to set the sled on the lip, front legs fully extended, and the back legs of the mount down the void. The various improvised mounts were much easier to move and conceal, though usually less stable and more difficult to adjust in terms of height.

Aiming

The MG 08 could be aimed for direct fire either by viewing through an 'optical' sight, or by means of the integral 'iron' sights. The usual optical sight was the Zilfernrohr 12, mounted to the left rear of the gun's receiver, giving 2.5× magnification. The sight was used:

Textbook usage of 'dragging straps' with the MG 08 sled mount folded, and the straps attached for short-range movement across flat terrain. From a commercial postcard sent by a member of an *Ersatz-Maschinengewehr-Kompagnie* with XIX. Armeekorps in September 1917.

1) To secure better definition of indistinct targets, especially at the long ranges, and in dull lights or moonlight, when laying over the ordinary sights would not be possible.

2) To meet special atmospheric conditions, such as mist, fog, snow, or very brilliant sunshine. For this two yellow glasses of different strengths are provided, which fit over the front lens. (General Staff 1918: 18)

With the range drum set at the estimated range, the gunner looked through the Zilfernrohr 12 and lined up what the Germans called the 'swallow tail' on target – in English, the view through the sight has usually been described as an 'arrow head' or 'inverted V' reticle. A cap protected the instrument's eyepiece when it was not in use. In transit the Zilfernrohr 12 was not usually left attached to the gun, but carried in a distinctively shaped leather case.

The MG 08 iron sights consisted of a simple forend post, offset to the left near the gun muzzle, and a rear bar or 'leaf' which popped up to vertical, and up and down which a 'V' notch slid to allow for range. The vertical scale was marked in 50m increments up to 2,000m. The firer set the range and lined up the notch and post on target. A steadied elevation was achieved by turning the metal handwheel at the base of the sled mount: clockwise for raising the muzzle, anticlockwise to depress it. For indirect fire, the basic method used for much of the war was to make sure the weapon was level, consult the range table and set elevation accordingly. Direction of aim relied on reference to landmarks, compass and map. From 1918, a dedicated 'indirect fire' kit was also produced for the MG 08. This comprised a dial sight to be mounted in place of the optical sight; a compass-type fire director to fit on the sled mount; and a protractor. Used in conjunction with a traverse-limitation bracket the team now had the means, at least in theory, to engage an unseen enemy over 3km away. Vagaries of weather, terrain, ammunition and crew skill meant that 'indirect fire' was only useful for 'area' targets, however, preferably using a large number of guns for saturation. The British Machine Gun Corps may have pioneered the 'machine gun barrage', but the Germans were not far behind, and were clearly using similar techniques during the latter part of 1917. Efforts were hampered less by lack of technical knowledge than by slow machine-gun production until 1916, and strategic situations dictating the use of a large proportion of available weapons in direct-fire roles.

To deal with immediate threats to a machine gun, the elevation handwheel of the MG 08 could be completely disengaged by means of a catch, allowing the gunner to move speedily, if less precisely, from target to target. Traverse of the MG 08 on its sled was limited to 30 degrees, far less than was possible with most tripod mounts. Nevertheless, this was adequate for most situations as it allowed for an arc of 100m when the target was 200m

A typical 2.5× optical sight for the MG 08 manufactured by Emil Busch. 'A' is the eyepiece, 'B' the range drum graduated in hundreds of metres, 'C' the front lens protected by its leather cap and 'D' the dovetailed base of the sight, which slid into a seating to the side of the gun breech. From General Staff 1918.

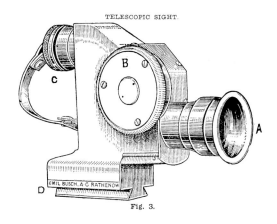

TELESCOPIC SIGHT.

EMIL BUSCH, A.G RATHENOW

Fig. 3.

from the gun. Traverse was accomplished by pushing or tapping the spade grips and the gun slid left or right on its rear mounting plate. A locking handle allowed the traverse to be clamped off in a predetermined position.

The MG 08/15 was usually fitted with iron sights only. The back sight was of the 'tangent' type – a ramp with an open 'V' notch raised and lowered by a slider – not unlike that seen on many rifles of the period. It was marked in 100m increments up to 2,000m, though such a maximum was very optimistic. The front sight was a small post offset to the firer's left. The firer simply swung the barrel across or up or down on the bipod to change target. Swift realigning of barrel onto target may have been assisted by the positioning of the bipod – well back under the barrel, but forward of the centre of gravity – but this arrangement had disadvantages. These included the need for the firer to keep his head fairly erect in order to both operate the trigger and take sight over the barrel, the propensity for the weapon to rock slightly, and for water in the jacket to slosh around during longer bursts.

Fire control

Ideally, fire control of MG 08 teams was by the controlling officer, relaying target, ranges and nature of fire to the NCOs. If the precise range was unknown, distance could be corrected by 'ranging fire' and adjusted or 'walked' onto the target. If this was not possible, as in a case where a group of guns were to open a surprise fire, different weapons could be set at 50m-range intervals, thereby spreading points of impact over a larger area. Hand or voice signals opened and ceased fire, though it was usually necessary for the gun commander, or the gun No. 1, to tap whoever was actually firing on the shoulder to stop, as commands were easily drowned out by the noise of the gun. Early in the war at least, no attempt was made to control the fire of companies brigaded together from a central position (Cron 2001: 122).

Rear view of an MG 08 fitted with its shield in a front-line position, *c.*1915. From this angle the sled mount elevating wheel, and the hand grips and trigger mechanism of the gun, are visible.

ON THE WORLD WAR I BATTLEFIELD

Early actions

Advice to the German machine-gun detachment of 1914 was that to shoot well at the opportune moment, having gunners full of initiative who were led by commanders with 'tactical insight' was the best guarantee of success. Teams were encouraged to take full advantage of ground, and measure or estimate distances as accurately as possible. In theory at least, guns were viable on any ground 'practicable for the infantry' and the target they presented in return was little greater than that offered by men in skirmish order; while an established machine-gun detachment had 'nothing to fear' from cavalry, they were advised not to engage 'well sheltered firing lines' of enemy infantry, this requiring an expenditure of ammunition out of proportion to the result, and often machine guns were better kept silent and ready for the 'decisive moment' (Longstaff & Atteridge 1917: 156–57). Artillery was the best antidote to enemy machine guns, and where German machine guns were called upon to engage artillery they were to be pushed as far forward as possible, preferably to flank an enemy battery. Machine-gun commanders were encouraged to think in terms of maximizing their own fire first, and maximizing cover second. As a rule it was expected that machine guns would be deployed 'about 20 paces' apart, though not evenly in line at equal intervals (Longstaff & Atteridge 1917: 159). Rather, individual weapons were to be located where they had best field of fire and best cover. Care was to be taken not to open fire prematurely, but to wait until a good target was presented at a good range. However, once fire was opened it had to be sustained until the effect sought was achieved. Shorter bursts of really effective fire had the greatest practical and moral impact on the enemy, while at the same time conserving ammunition.

Basic tactical use of the machine gun was summarized in a privately produced Prussian manual of 1915:

> Lying behind the gun the Richtschütz [gun No. 2] presses the trigger piece and the gun gives an unbroken succession of 250 shots, a belt in 30 to 40 seconds. Fire can be interrupted at any time. Delivery of a single shot is

The MG 08 in the First Battle of the Aisne, 1914 (overleaf)

The deployment of machine guns was shocking to both sides early in the war, especially during attacks on prepared positions, when superior numbers were frequently stopped in their tracks by a combination of rifle and machine-gun fire. Inspired by contemporary photos, a British sketch (in General Staff 1914b) and German descriptions of field works (in Reichskriegsministerium 1911), we see here details of a German position on the Aisne in September 1914. Freshly dug trenches, not yet connected into a continuous line, are supported by machine-gun pits. Some are in the front line with fields of fire to both front and side; others are completely concealed behind the first line firing 'en enfilade' between the infantry trenches, sweeping the ground in front.

possible, but in combat not advisable. The fire effect of a machine gun is equivalent to a war strength infantry platoon. The fire pattern is, however, about three times denser than that of the infantry. The fire effect must also be greater if it is possible to bring it on target. The combat use of the MG company is by platoons, alone, or as part of the line.

Guns may move so long as they are out of sight of the enemy. Whenever the MGs come in sight, or range of the enemy, they and their ammunition must be prepared. The MG is carried or drawn by two other ranks. Two other men carry two ammunition boxes each. In each box are 500 rounds ready for use lined up in long belts. The NCO is the gun commander, his function being equivalent to that of a section commander.

Frequently the machine guns go forward with the firing line. In order that this not be made known to the enemy the weapon is taken apart and hurried up to the line in two pieces. Between the two MGs of a platoon a width of 20 paces is maintained. The squads situated to the right and left of the gun fall under command of the machine gun officer. They must help pick up and haul ammunition if machine gunners fall hors de combat. The ammunition boxes are carried by means of Tragegurten ['carry belts' or 'dragging straps'], one of which is worn running over the shoulder of each gunner. The straps are attached to the handles of the boxes, and the covers of the guns are closed. On the position the boxes are positioned to the right near the guns; pointing forwards. The infantrymen who have brought up ammunition boxes shoot from the position with their own arms. (Klaß 1915: 219–21)

Both the machine-gun company and the two-gun platoon were regarded as tactical units in their own right, even in 1914. They were also distinct from artillery, doing their best work at much closer ranges, as the British *Handbook of the German Army* observed:

Machine guns are not intended to replace artillery. Their effective range is 2,200 yards [2,010m], and it is realised in Germany that about 1,500 yards [1,370m] is the useful machine gun action. No hard and fast rules are laid down as to the massing or dispersing the guns of a battery or company; but though guns are often used in pairs, it is rare to hear of a gun being used singly. The tendency is to keep the six guns massed. (General Staff 1914a: 122)

Earlier wars had seen occasions when mass attacks were stopped by overwhelming firepower, but the Maxim took this to a new level in 1914. As eyewitness Karl von Wiegand reported of the battle of Wirballen in Russian Poland (now Lithuania):

For the first time I sensed the intoxication of battle ... On came the Slav swarm – into the range of the German trenches, with wild yells and never a waver. Russian battle flags – the first I had seen – appeared in front of the charging ranks. The advance line thinned and the second line moved up. Nearer and nearer they swept towards the German positions. And then came a new sight! A few seconds later came a new sound. First I saw

a sudden, almost grotesque, melting of the advancing lines. It was different to anything that had taken place before. The men literally went down like dominoes in a row. Those who kept their feet were hurled back as though by a terrible gust of wind. Almost in the second that I pondered, puzzled, the staccato rattle of machine guns reached us. My ear answered the query of my eye. For the first time the advancing lines hesitated, apparently bewildered. Mounted officers dashed along the line urging men forward. Horses fell with men. I saw a dozen riderless horses dashing madly through the lines, adding a new terror. Another horse was obviously running away with his officer rider. The crucial period for the section of the charge on which I had riveted my attention probably lasted less than a minute. To my throbbing brain it seemed an hour. Then, with the withering fire raking them, even as they faltered, the lines broke. Panic ensued. It was every man for himself. The entire Russian charge turned and went tearing back to cover ... (Quoted in Bull 2007: 23)

A gun team carry an MG 08 stretcherwise with a man at either end of the sled. The soldier to the left brings up two 500-round ammunition boxes, while the man to the right holds the water can. Three of the team are equipped with dragging straps.

During the Battle of the Frontiers in the West there were similar incidents on both sides, and the need to attack and use machine guns at the same time presented particular tactical problems. The British were of course keen to learn how German machine guns were moved and deployed, and a report from a 'private individual travelling in Belgium' in August and September 1914 appeared in the very first edition of *Notes from the Front* (General Staff 1914b: 36). According to this intelligence the German infantry were being used essentially as 'a support for artillery and for the machine gun', and mobile machine gun units were pushed forward in the advance; a 'spectator' added the interesting detail that some weapons were conveyed longer distances either nine to a motor lorry, or in threes on horse-drawn carts (General Staff 1914b: 36–37). In the latter instance two men rode with each gun, and an NCO or junior officer served as outrider.

> The members of this mobile machine gun force march light, their knapsacks, blankets, and in some cases their rifles, being carried in

their carts. The mounted men that accompany them have a rope and leather harness, so that the horse can be used as the leader of a tandem in case of heavy going. The cart has strong and steady springs. The appearance of the cart, with in its load of, in some cases, bundles of forage, knapsacks, haversacks and blankets, would not attract the slightest attention. The guns at the bottom were absolutely hidden. The cart is somewhat like an English butcher's cart, only much heavier. The tail board drops down in the ordinary way. (General Staff 1914b: 37)

Jäger battalions with their own machine-gun companies and ten-vehicle 'motorised columns' were initially attached to the cavalry and so were well forward; in all cases, the usefulness of having machine guns 'up with the regiment' was apparent, and having been unloaded from carts or lorries they were man-hauled, individual guns being seen 'carried in the manner of an African hammock on the shoulders of bearers' (General Staff 1914b: 37). Others were carried like a stretcher, 'with a blanket thrown over the gun and a couple of knapsacks or perhaps an ammunition box': in such instances the gunners 'at a distance are easily mistaken for stretcher bearers carrying a wounded man off the field' (General Staff 1914b: 37). It was even claimed that in case of danger machine guns were wrapped in blankets and buried, crews returning to retrieve them later.

Trench warfare

Arguably, the machine gun quickly became even more important in defending trenches and field works – what German manuals called 'position warfare'. Initially, machine guns were placed in the front line or within the main position, but by mid-1915 it had become more usual to position them behind the front line. As the Somme battle approached, a key document

A very posed photograph purporting to show '2. Rekrut-Korporalschaft of II. Ersatz-Maschinengewehr-Kompagnie, shooting enemy fliers', at Saarlouis, September 1915. The recruits, clad in fatigue uniform, use the MG 08 *Hauptschild* (gun shield) to achieve elevation. The weapon itself appears to have a patched water jacket, often the result of combat damage.

governing the use of German machine guns was captured and translated into English as *Regulations for Machine Gun Officers and Non Commissioned Officers* (General Staff 1916c). Perhaps unsurprisingly, given the impending Franco-British attack on the Somme, these regulations focused upon defensive deployment. Ideally, guns were provided with emplacements, kept in such condition as to allow the weapon to cover 'the whole prescribed field of fire' (General Staff 1916c). Nearby were to be two alternative emplacements covering a similar part of the terrain. These three positions were for use in the event of an enemy attack, but in order to prevent discovery at other times firing took place from elsewhere, and was directed so as not to damage wire entanglements. Additional observation posts, preferably close enough to allow viewing with the naked eye, were positioned to overlook enemy trenches and ground behind.

Immediate ammunition supply was 16 boxes (4,000 rounds) per gun, and as soon as a box was exhausted a replacement was brought up from the belt store. Checking the store was a daily task for the platoon commander, but keeping the belts dry was the duty of the gun No. 1, who took damp belts into the dugouts to dry them, though without exposure to any direct heat from a stove – wet or rapidly dried belts might otherwise shrink, stretch or distort. The last 2,500 rounds for any gun were considered the 'iron ration', but as soon as the store dropped below 5,000, this was reported to the sector machine-gun officer who immediately indented to the company commander for more. Other items kept on hand included three spare barrels for the gun, a tool case and a barrel of water. While stoppages were cleared by the gun crew, repairs were the province of the sector armoury where chisels, files and larger items were kept.

Given the ever-present danger of raids and close assault, gun positions were furnished with personal arms and signal equipment. The signal pistol with each gun was supplied with 35 flare cartridges (20 white, ten red and five green), and a further 20 cartridges were kept in the store. At night one of the sentries was to carry a flare pistol and ammunition. Other pistols

Württemberg infantrymen heave an MG 08 up into its trench firing position, *c.*1916. The gun has just the flip-up iron sight, and is fitted with both the water-jacket front armour and a trench mount in the form of a folding under-barrel tripod. At the forend is the Rückstoßverstärker 08S muzzle booster for use with ball ammunition.

53

were carried loaded, but without a round in the chamber, and with a spare magazine in the belt pouch. Other members of the team would often remain in the dugouts, but were expected to appear in their equipment and carrying gasmasks when emerging. Only at night were those guarding the machine gun with semi-automatics allowed a round in the chamber, with the safety on. Six grenades – a crucial weapon of last resort – were kept with each machine gun, and in each dugout, a further ten being in the store. All small arms were to be checked weekly by the gun No. 1, and by snap inspection by officers at other times. Rifles, pistols and grenades were to be kept clean, bayonets slightly greased against rust.

Machine-gun sentries were posted one during the day, but two at night, each being provided with a periscope. In the event of an attack, or the enemy offering an exceptional target, the sentries were to sound an alarm, audible within the crew dugouts. These alarms were tested daily by the machine-gunners, and frequently by platoon commanders and sector machine-gun officers. The team scrambled to their weapon as quickly as possible, the time taken being recorded during practices. Different soundings of alarms were to signify gas or the onset of bombardment, with the gun team trained to take appropriate action. During the night the gun was kept loaded and ready in one of the emplacements, while during the day it was placed at the foot of the dugout steps, together with a box of ammunition. By this time the gun was 'always mounted on the extemporised mounting [trench mount]', the sled mount being reserved only for occasions when 'extremely accurate shooting is required' (General Staff 1916c).

Guns were registered in advance on special targets within their field of fire, and a record kept of targets and ranges. The record card had a standard arrangement with targets listed right to left across the field of view, and by map square and distance. Brief descriptions and remarks were also included. The gun No. 1 was authorized to open fire whenever the enemy attacked, or on sighting a particularly favourable target. In the event of such an engagement the gunner reported his action immediately to the platoon commander and section machine-gun officer. Gun teams were to be informed whenever friendly troops were out in front; nevertheless, they were still to open fire in the event of enemy attack.

Some weapons were also detailed for anti-aircraft duties, and mounted accordingly, a three-man team remaining constantly on hand during the hours of daylight, with their machine gun loaded. One of the three men took sentry duty, and

An anti-aircraft gun team using an MG 08 on a camouflaged extemporized mounting, c.1917. A cartwheel is attached so as to revolve on a post, with the weight of the gun and sled balanced by the water can and a bucket of soil attached to the opposite side of the wheel rim.

on sighting enemy aircraft alerted the others. Normal action was to engage when the enemy was within 1,500m, laying a 'vertical searching fire' 20 lengths ahead of the aircraft (General Staff 1916c). If the enemy got through, the gun was swung and re-laid to fire again ahead of the plane.

A couple of months later, on 3 September 1916, 6. Bayerische Infanterie-Division, which fought at both Verdun and the Somme, issued its own update to the regulations, pointing out that

> The Battle of the Somme has again shown the decisive value of machine guns in defence. If they can be kept in serviceable condition until the enemy's infantry attacks and are then brought up into the firing position in time, every attack must fail. The greater the efforts the enemy makes in the future to destroy our trenches before his assault by an increased expenditure of ammunition, the greater the extent to which we must rely on machine guns for repulsing attacks. These should be brought into action unexpectedly and continue the fight when the greater part of the garrison of the front line trenches is out of action, and the enemy's barrage fire renders it difficult to bring up reinforcements. (General Staff 1916b: 1)

Guns were only left in the first-line trenches when deployed in dugouts with several exits, and from which the machine guns could be brought out in time to meet the attack. Owing to the difficulty of observing attacks in time, many machine guns were to be put 'as a rule' behind the second trench, or better still, the third, since enemy bombardment was less effective here. The remainder of the Bavarian machine guns were to be

A machine-gun officer and men with an MG 08, sled mount folded, on a handcart, *c.*1917. During the war, six carts were issued per *Maschinengewehr-Kompagnie* for man-hauling guns, ammunition and equipment. A T-shaped handle at the front end allowed two men to pull the cart with relative ease on roads.

behind the trench system and on ground further in the rear, in deep pits which are usually covered over and also on platforms concealed in trees, in such a manner the enemy is caught in an unexpected cross fire if he breaks through. The important point is that the machine guns should not, in any circumstances, be detected beforehand. They must not, therefore, be too close to trenches which can be photographed, or to well defined woods which the enemy will suspect in any case. The best sites are therefore in the open [though presumably concealed by folds in the ground or pits], in or under clumps of trees and bushes, or in hedges. All the earth excavated must be removed or concealed under hedges, etc. A low network of trip wires has proved to be the best form of obstacle. To each machine gun should be allotted a certain number of infantrymen armed with hand grenades, who can also work the gun if necessary. (General Staff 1916b: 1)

Time-consuming dedicated machine-gun emplacements were deemed inadvisable, as they attracted fire, and the weapons themselves were best used from 'improvised mountings or from sandbags' (General Staff 1916b: 1). While the presence of machine guns gave a significant boost – moral as well as practical – to German defence, gunners were under considerable pressure not just to respond swiftly to the threat of attack, but to cope with the danger posed by return fire from an enemy that had learned to regard machine guns as a priority target. As machine-gunner E. Reubke observed:

> It can easily all go wrong, for when they have found out a machine gun position for a start, they let loose on us with all their weapons, since machine guns are really terrible arms. One wouldn't know until experiencing the impact of such a weapon working on its most powerful level while lying behind it. The whole work takes place on the ground – mainly these 30 seconds of the most fabulous work and hurry until the machine gun is in position and ready to fire – and then the handicraft of murder starts. It must be a very strange feeling to lie behind a machine gun shooting at infantry troops moving forward. One can see them coming and directs this terrible hail against them. (Quoted in Ulrich 2010: 75)

With the continuing attrition of trench warfare, and the ever-present danger from artillery, German defence came to rely ever more heavily on machine guns. This was because interlocking zones of fire presented not only a formidable, and often deadly, impediment to the attack, but economized on manpower with a handful of sentries, snipers and machine-gunners doing the duty of whole companies of riflemen. Remarkably, a direct connection was made between the reduction of Western Front infantry-battalion establishments to 750 men, and the issue of three light machine guns per company. Moreover, supporting evidence that this was not just fanciful thinking came from estimates of ammunition expenditure now suggesting that in various engagements the machine guns fired anywhere between two-thirds and nine-tenths of the total small-arms rounds used by German forces (General Staff 1917b: 1.27).

Stellungsbau (Reichskriegsministerium 1916), the new German defence manual of November 1916, emphasized 'strong points', 'back stops' and deep positions. Critically, 'Machine gun posts and dugouts' were to form the 'framework' of all infantry fighting lines. These positions did not necessarily require long and unobstructed fields of fire, for weapons could be deployed or redeployed to cover gaps from concealed positions, or to provide enfilade fire from ranges as short as 100m. While purpose-built machine-gun emplacements and concrete works were common, often on reverse slopes to avoid fire, many weapons were simply stowed in cubby-holes under the forward lip of trenches and pits until needed. Where resources allowed, such stores could themselves be hardened with concrete.

By April 1917 British intelligence was able to observe that

> At the present stage of operations one of the enemy's chief methods of defence consists in holding strong points immediately in rear of his defensive systems. These strong points usually contain one or more machine guns and are arranged chequer-wise so as to be mutually supporting. They are frequently concealed in hollows so as to be difficult to detect from the air and for artillery to deal with ... On being compelled to fall back from any organised system of defence, the enemy usually does so covered by small infantry rearguards which hold tactical points. These rearguards are, as a rule, armed with machine guns. (General Staff 1917a: 1)

Possible answers to such tactics were suggested: first, to push forward 'small tactical advanced guards' (General Staff 1917a: 1), then to engage the German machine guns. Where the defence was well organized this was done by artillery, with friendly machine guns to cover the advance of infantry and mortars. British machine-gun crews were instructed to engage the Germans 'by cross fire' from two or more subsections of machine guns, sweeping the 'suspected locality' by means of either direct or indirect fire; the infantry themselves were to open fire with Lewis guns from the 'nearest cover available' (General Staff 1917a: 1). Almost inevitably, this would cause the German machine gunner to turn his attention, 'and owing to the apparently limited traverse of the German machine gun, it may then be possible for the other sections to work round either flank and to get within range of their particular weapons' (General Staff 1917a: 2). Riflemen aimed to get onto the flank, and attack with fire or the bayonet, while the Stokes mortar, pushed well forward, would cause a 'moral effect' (General Staff 1917a: 2). Smoke laid by artillery or mortars could mask the German gun, making the approach safer.

'MG post number 14' during a realistic exercise, c.1917. The NCO gun commander, left, is equipped with field glasses and pistol; the gun has an optical sight and armoured barrel jacket. In front of the ammunition box is the small oblong water can.

As so often during the conflict, tactical innovation led to tactical counterstroke, and so it was with the deployment of machine guns. As German instructions issued in the wake of the fighting against the French on the Aisne during 1917 explained:

> Machine guns should only exceptionally be posted in the front line. Emplacements should be inconspicuous, and tunnels (including the entrances), well camouflaged. There should be no machine gun nests, for the latter will be detected by aeroplanes, and destroyed by the artillery. No firing should take place before the infantry attack. The employment of massed machine gun companies is to be recommended. Zones of machine guns should be formed between the second and third lines, the guns being sited according to the field of fire obtainable. These zones of machine guns should be reinforced by light Minenwerfer and Granatenwerfer. The supply of ammunition in belts should be ample, at least 4,000 rounds per gun. (General Staff 1917b: 3.13)

A machine-gun team in the latter part of World War I with an MG 08 on a Gebirgslafette ('alpine mount') 16 mounting. The mountain tripod, often carried by horse or mule, had adjustable legs, and was smaller and lighter than the sled.

Moreover, instructions for the tactical use of the MG 08/15 were different again, and indeed much more like those applied to the Lewis gun. According to 6. Armee orders of 1917, the ideal battle crew of the MG 08/15 was three, all of whom were advised to carry a carbine as well, 'in order that these three men should not be completely lost for combat in case the machine gun should not work' (US War Department 1918: 18). In defence, the MG 08/15 team was to be close to the platoon commander, concealed in the first line, perhaps using a shell crater or forward sap, and so positioned as to provide flanking fire across ground also swept by another gun from a different angle. Given the unsuitability of the weapon

for overhead fire, it was only to be positioned between the first and second lines in exceptional circumstances. Maximum advantage could be had of the gun's mobility in defence by frequent changes of position. The MG 08/15 would not 'replace' the MG 08, but with bursts of harassing fire and the engagement of 'momentary targets' and enemy assaults, much increase the fire capacity of the infantry (US War Department 1918: 19).

In the attack the MG 08/15 was to be used with 'a certain spirit of initiative' (US War Department 1918: 19), going forward with the front line and focusing its fire on parts of the enemy trench which held up the attack. Being near the platoon commander, it could quickly be thrown into action exactly where needed. In 'small enterprises' the weapon could be stationed to a flank, supporting as needed, but only moving onto captured ground 'when the bomb fighting has ended' (US War Department 1918: 20). Being established in an enemy position, its task was to protect the flanks and stop enemy counter-attacks, but in these circumstances it was 'absolutely indispensable' to have the MG 08/15 protected by 'special details of bombers'(US War Department 1918: 20).

The light machine gun was perfectly capable of being used in offensive operations, even if this entailed 'some dragging' (US War Department 1918: 20), and – with the avoidance of continuous fire – an immediate ammunition supply of 1,200–1,500 cartridges was deemed adequate. No battle use beyond 5,000 rounds had yet been reported. In the example given of the attack on the French holding Cepy Farm, two or three light machine guns were placed in the second wave of each company, the first wave of the attack being composed of *Stoßtruppen* (shock troops) and *Pioniere* (combat engineers) in little groups as small as eight to ten men.

In action, the MG 08/15s were to fall under the infantry commander, regimental machine-gun officers having only the duty of after-battle care of weapons. Individual gunners were trained in dealing with stoppages, but also had to learn how to bring their weapons to bear quickly in shell holes 'without letting the barrel touch the edge of the crater'; change locks and barrels in the bottom of the hole; crawl with the gun; and 'spring from one shell crater to another carrying the machine gun slung over the shoulder' (US War Department 1918: 21). Gunners were to act promptly and on their own initiative, and to execute drills in detail in concert with infantry.

The *Maschinengewehr-Hilfslafette* screwed into the top of a post to adapt the MG 08 for anti-aircraft fire. Drawing from Merkatz 1917 & 1918.

Die M.G.-Hilfslafette.

Bild 18.

Die M.G.-Hilfslafette.

AFTER WORLD WAR I

German machine guns played a significant role during the 'last hundred days' of World War I, frequently being used as a mechanism to create delays and cover the retreat, as Canadian machine-gun officer Lieutenant-Colonel C.S. Grafton recalled:

> The German machine gunner had invariably shown himself to be the pick of the enemy troops – fighting his gun to the bitter end. And it was usually the bitter end, for the qualities of mercy had been pretty well strained to breaking point by the time the attacking troops had reached the source of so much of their trouble and from which flamed forth so much death in their ranks. (Quoted in Cornish 2009: 74)

Nor was this a message lost on the victorious powers. As a result, stiff demands were imposed on the German arsenal as part of the terms of the Armistice of November 1918. The surrender of 25,000 machine guns 'in good condition' formed part of Clause 4 of the terms presented by Maréchal Ferdinand Foch's delegation. With the Treaty of Versailles in 1919, and the limitation of the German Army to ten divisions, more exacting restrictions were applied. The allowance was 'up to' 108 heavy and 162 light machine guns per infantry division, with the total for all seven infantry divisions not to exceed 756 heavy and 1,134 light; an additional 12 heavy machine guns were permitted for each of three cavalry divisions, making a total of 792 heavy and 1,134 light. Ammunition stock for machine guns was set at 15,408,000 rounds.

A 1930s postcard from the 'Unser Wehrmacht' series showing an MG 08 firing. The gun commander, right, carries the case for the optical sight; the water can is centre foreground.

While German machine guns were undoubtedly much reduced in number, it appears that quite a few more were actually retained than were permitted by treaty terms. Indeed, there was some alarm in 1920 when Allied governments became aware that German war materials, including 25,000 machine guns, had been exported to the Netherlands. Other

Machine-gunners march behind a steel-bodied lf 3 machine-gun wagon, c.1939. This two-wheeled vehicle carried two weapons, and was towed behind a limber pulled by two horses. In the left-hand file the first marching man carries a binocular case, the second a pouch for an optical sight for the machine gun.

weapons were already there, having been surrendered by units crossing the neutral Dutch border late in 1918. It was feared that the Germans would benefit financially by these methods of disposal, or – worse – gain access to such weapons at some future date. Some weapons were probably also unaccounted for in the hands of paramilitaries.

German training literature of the 1920s described the light machine gun as the most important weapon the infantry possessed for the firefight. While the extended crew was four, the gunner (the No. 2 in the German system of the moment) aimed and fired the weapon. He had to be trained not only to shoot but to use all forms of terrain and cover to advantage; have good knowledge of stoppages; achieve surprise and open fire quickly, and to manhandle the gun carrying it, and working it, even in a gasmask. As of 1921 a machine-gun team was regarded as a squad, working within a mixed platoon. As such the MG 08/15 was therefore to cooperate both with nearby rifle squads and the heavy machine guns. In the attack it was to go well forward, just behind the scouts. In the event of a team being spotted by the enemy, it was likely to draw fire and have to relocate, preferably taking advantage of covering fire from other guns. In the defence the light machine gun was likewise to cooperate with other weapons, suitably protected against ground and air observation. Very possibly it could break up enemy attacks, focusing its fire by surprise on any short-range bunched targets of advancing infantry. It could not be expected to engage at long ranges where artillery and heavy machine guns were to do their work, however, nor to deal with single infantrymen who might be better targets for snipers with telescopic sights. *In extremis*, if their retreat was compromised, MG 08/15 crews could be expected to fight to the last cartridge, taking recourse to grenades and sidearms, or picking up the rifles of fallen comrades. During manoeuvres, the potential importance of MGs was by no means underestimated, the 1924 regulations laying down that at 800 metres the effective fire of rifles and light machine guns together could expect to achieve 'annihilating effect' (Reichskriegsministerium 1928: 58). Heavy machine guns were deemed very effective at 1,200m and useful at 2,500m (fired directly) and 3,500m (fired indirectly).

That the terms of the Treaty of Versailles allowed the cavalry only a very few heavy machine guns was especially bemoaned. German experts opined that the mounted arm should be able to do everything the infantry was capable of, and its reconnaissance detachments lacked the firepower required to drive off an enemy without light machine guns being brought swiftly into action. Ideally, it was recommended that every cavalry troop should have six weapons mounted on pack animals. This would be in addition to a heavy-machine-gun troop of 12 guns attached to each cavalry regiment, and a whole machine-gun battalion for each cavalry brigade. Needless to say this was not achieved, though exercises at Döberitz in 1926 experimented with a thin cavalry skirmish line heavily reinforced with machine guns, one heavy and two light guns every 100m. This was deemed capable of holding up a large number of infantry for several hours until the latter could bring up double this number of machine guns, and so force the cavalry back. In another foray a cavalry unit practised work around the flank of an infantry attack and bringing it under fire with machine guns.

The post-war period also saw efforts to get better performance out of the weapons left to the truncated Reichswehr. In 1923, for example, Major Paul Hausser attempted to promote the development of indirect fire, observing that prior to 1914 very little had been done about unobserved fire, but noting that – spurred by the British and the French – the subject had been promoted very rapidly in the latter part of the war. Arguments he now put forward for the advancement of indirect fire included the desirability of concealment and surprise, the possibility of keeping guns in the same place for longer, and – since indirect fire teams did not need to see their targets – the fact that shooting could be continued at night or in any weather condition. Naturally there were limits, since close-range indirect fire was often impossible with relatively flat-trajectory weapons, observation of effect was difficult, and to plaster a target thoroughly enough to ensure hits required large quantities of ammunition. In 1924 Oberst Stollberger focused attention on infantry combat, and drills to be adopted in the face of specific enemy weapons. In one exercise an infantry battalion was subjected to a notional air attack and was taught to react by breaking down into small units, spread out so as not to offer any good targets, with the light machine guns firing bursts, aiming slightly ahead of the lead aircraft.

In any event, for the time being the MG 08 and MG 08/15, supplemented by the MG 08/18, continued to be the main issue machine guns of Germany's armed forces. This would remain the case until the MG 13 was further developed, being tested in the USSR in 1927, and produced in numbers not long afterward. The MG 34, a much better all-round weapon, was developed

A machine-gun wagon drawn by six horses is pulled into position, mid-1930s. Horse-drawn heavy-machine-gun sections remained on German infantry establishments to the end of World War II.

in the early 1930s, and re-equipped the front-line infantry of the expanding Heer (Army) prior to World War II. Even then, however, the MG 08 and MG 08/15 were retained, as for example in local defence roles and reserves. The MG 08 was kept by the Landwehr, and the MG 08/15 saw a new lease of life, being widely deployed in the anti-aircraft role.

According to the 1928 document *Die Schießgestelle für MG 08*, three main types of mount were now current for the MG 08. These were the old sled mount, the tripod and the expedient 'auxiliary *Lafette*'. Both sled mount and tripod could be used with an extension tube to produce a simple anti-aircraft pintle, and both these mountings were to be painted overall with camouflage paint, excepting only vital working parts. These included the elevation and traverse limiters, and the clamp assembly, which were blued or black, and the glide path which was left bare steel. The elevation plate and fire table were chromed. Both tripod and sled were deemed suitable for 'the delivery of effective burst fire with direct or indirect aiming techniques up to 3,500 m distance'; interestingly, it was noted that the 'tripod has the advantage over the four legged sled that all of the legs always rest on the ground, and that it allows the MG a greater traverse' (Reichskriegsministerium 1928: 9 & 29).

The 'auxiliary *Lafette*', by contrast, was now described only as a 'rough and ready' mount (Reichskriegsministerium 1928: 55), suffering considerable dispersion of fire and by consequence being suitable only for use against air and ground targets at ranges up to 500m. Against such limited performance, the auxiliary mounting was seen to offer some advantages, being smaller, lighter, much easier to conceal and able to pivot through 360 degrees; moreover, it was equally useful with the MG 08/15.

As in World War I, the auxiliary mount was recommended to be attached to a small wooden board for field use, so spreading the ground weight and allowing the piece to revolve. For anti-aircraft work it was fixed on 'a stump, pole, or dug in post' (Reichskriegsministerium 1928: 55), around which there was freedom of movement for the crew. The ideal position was in the bottom of a shell crater, firmly affixed to a stout wooden post 1.5m high, with the top of the post level with the lip of the pit. When this could be achieved the gun was perfectly placed for the crew to fire skywards, sweeping and tracking enemy aircraft. Conversely, it was still possible to engage in ground fire in defence of the pit.

For both the heavy and light weapons, a number of modifications were introduced. These included a new type of feeder capable of taking either canvas or metal belts. A 'squeeze trigger' was also devised, and fitted to at least some MG 08s. Yet the most significant changes were made to the MG 08/15, many examples of which were now equipped with an anti-aircraft sight, a modified buttstock assembly, and a forward bipod-mounting bracket. This last change, supporting the weapon close to the muzzle rather than further back, was designed to improve stability and thus accuracy. It also had the knock-on effect of altering the firer's posture and technique, creating an arc of traverse that was effectively smaller. While minor adjustments were arguably easier, to change aim very significantly the gunner had to move his body around, or reposition the gun.

Nevertheless, official manuals such as *Schießvorschrift* (Reichskriegsministerium 1931) and *Die Maschinengewehre 08/15 und 08/18* (Reibert 1933) often showed guns with the bipod still mounted towards the rear of the barrel jacket. Interwar photos also depicted MG 08/15s being used in conjunction with a tripod, though this rather defeated

A second-line unit still using MG 08 machine guns on old sled mountings, 1940.

the notion of specialist heavy and light Maxims, rather than creating a genuine 'general purpose' weapon. The belt feeder conversion programme for MG 08 types was never completed, apparently being abandoned as attention focused on production of the new MG 34. Interestingly, a photograph exists in the Imperial War Museum collections showing an MG 08/15 captured by British troops during the French campaign of 1940. On this weapon the bipod is shown fitted to the rear bracket, despite the gun also having the forward bracket, and the gun also has features such as a late-type drum bracket and a tubular metal oil bottle set into the butt.

Remarkably, neither the MG 08 nor the MG 08/15 would completely disappear from the inventory of the German armed forces until the final surrender of May 1945. As new weapons such as the MG 34 and MG 42 were produced and went to the front in ever increasing numbers, demand also spiralled as new forces were raised, and guns were lost or damaged in combat. The old Maxims therefore continued in limited service. Moreover, familiarity with the system was found indefinitely useful as various types of Maxim were captured from the enemy and also pressed into service, these being described for the benefit of German service personnel in a series of information leaflets. These 'foreign' guns encountered with German forces in a new World War included not only large numbers of Russian Model 1905 and Model 1910 Maxims, but German guns which had found their way to other countries prior to 1939. Among them were Yugoslav MG 08/15s, Belgian MG 08s and MG 08/15s, and Polish MG 08s. So it was that the MG 08 and other Maxims saw action even in the last days of World War II in the ruins of Berlin.

An MG 08/15 anti-aircraft gun team, late 1942. Though the carry sling is retained, the gun is mounted on a tall tripod of the type issued in the 1930s, and fitted with the large ring sight. When aircraft attacked head on, the gunner put the enemy at the centre of the ring. Crossing, diving and climbing targets were lined up at the appropriate edge of the ring so 'aiming off', i.e. allowing for the forward movement of the aircraft.

IMPACT
The 'beaten zone'

'The machine gunner may be likened to the fireman with his hose-pipe, whose object is to bring the base of his jet of water to play on a certain spot some distance away from the nozzle of his pipe,' reflected R.V.K. Applin in 1910.

> He does not trouble about the distance, he does not require to know the range; but pointing the nozzle in the direction of the spot he desires to strike, he elevates or depresses it until he observes the base of the cone of water falling on the right spot, and then he holds his pipe so that it continues to fall where he desires; he does not trouble about the smaller streams and drops of water that fall short or go beyond, but devotes his whole attention to keeping the nucleus of the stream – the 75 per cent, or 50 per cent, zone – falling on his 'target'. In precisely the same way the machine gunner must look upon his stream of bullets as a stream of water from a hose-pipe, and his object must be to cause the centre of that stream to play on the target, or, in other words, to bring the effective cone of fire on the target so that it is the centre of the beaten zone. This can be done by 'observing' the strike of the nucleus of the shots and altering the elevation accordingly. On favourable ground fire can be observed by No. 1 up to 800 yards [730m], but No. 2 with the aid of good glasses can observe fire on favourable ground up to 1,500 [1,370m]. This observation of fire is the best method of obtaining the correct elevation at 'effective' ranges (i.e. 1,400 to 600) [1,280m to 550m], if the ground is suitable. (Applin 1910: 33–34)

In absolute terms more Entente soldiers fell to German artillery than to German machine guns. Nevertheless, the machine gun was the defence weapon par excellence, and very often the devastation it caused was concentrated in time and space upon human targets at their most vulnerable: when attempting to advance. Machine guns had shorter range than artillery, but at the same time could be used with greater precision and economy to deny part of the battlefield to the enemy. Where zones of fire from guns hit the ground, 'beaten zones' were created where infantry movement was extremely hazardous, if not suicidal. These were intensified where fire from different machine guns overlaid or intersected. As early as 1915, German experts were recommending 'Advancing under MG fire is only possible by squads creeping or in small irregular jumps. When opportunity occurs, advancing from the flank or rear is successful' (Klaß 1915: 221). Engaging enemy machine guns with machine-gun fire was likewise most likely to succeed when crossfire was used. When such advice was ignored, or machine guns achieved surprise, the result could be devastation, with a couple of well-placed weapons perfectly capable of holding off a battalion.

Despite the fact that both the MG 08 and Gew 98 infantry rifle were sighted to 2,000m, and their bullets flew about the same distance overall, the machine gun was very much more effective at longer ranges. Indeed, indirect MG fire was possible out to as far as 4,000m, and manuals of the interwar period speak of 'effective burst fire' to 3,500m. The reason for this apparent contradiction was that the stability of the machine-gun mounting created a much tighter concentration of rounds than did a group of riflemen, who perforce fired from slightly different positions, with differing levels of skill, and from different rifles. This concentration of machine-gun rounds was what Merkatz dubbed the 'sheaf' of fire, often described by English speakers as the 'cone' of fire.

A postcard from 'Johannes' in the Champagne, 1918. The sender was a member of an MG 08/15 team: note the pistols for close defence, web dragging straps, 250-round belt boxes and water can. The gun commander, with the field glasses, wears the ribbon of the Iron Cross Second Class.

According to Merkatz (writing in *New Methods of Machine Gun Fire*), the cone of fire from the MG 08, when its barrel was properly clamped in the sled mount, was approximately 1m wide at 1,000m. The cone could be directed onto the target as *Punktfeuer* ('point fire'), *Tiefenfeuer* ('deep fire'), or *Breitenfeuer* ('broad fire'): that is, at one specific point, distributed in depth, or across a target. In virtually every instance the beaten zone created by the cone of fire of the machine gun was more effective than the equivalent area swept by infantry fire:

> The beaten zone of a poorly trained infantry company is even in peace greater [in area and more diffuse] than that of a well-trained one. While under the disintegrating influences of battle, the infantry beaten zone is materially enlarged, that of the machine gun will even in action deviate little or not at all from its peace dimensions. The so-called loss of nerve control does not appear here to the same extent, because being protected by the cover of the gun and in some cases by the shield, etc., the gun aimer is not subjected to the same extent to the influences of battle. With 100 or 200 m. deep fire, the new method of firing is so robust that even any loss of nerve control which results in displacement of the beaten zone through aiming errors, but as just stated, not in an enlargement of the zone would be neutralised. The commander has it in his hands to adapt the extent of deep fire to service conditions. (Merkatz 1916: 2–3)

In Merkatz's opinion, deviation of fire from the centre of the cone was less likely to be the result of failure of the firer, than the type and solidity of the gun mounting, or barrel wear. Automatic fire, properly used, was a methodical covering of areas, rather than a question of hitting a precise spot with an individual round:

The effect of range on trajectory and the size of beaten zones (Reichskriegsministerium 1937). As distance to target increases, the gun needs to be elevated to reach its mark, and the bullet path is no longer flat. The result is a reduction in the area of the beaten zone, which is no longer a large extended 'cone' but a much smaller elongated oval.

> The term, 'chance hits', sometimes does a good deal of harm. One may even maintain that every shot, not called as a bull's-eye, is a chance hit. I differ. A hit within a systematically laid sheaf [cone of fire] is not a chance hit, but is based on calculation. If we fire with a machine gun against small targets at 1000 meters, with sight set at 1050 meters

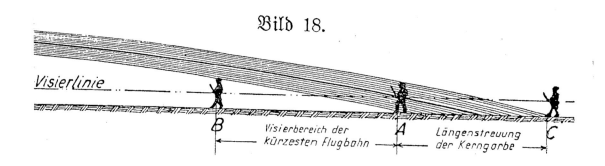

Bild 18.

Visierlinie

B   Visierbereich der
        kürzesten Flugbahn   A   Längenstreuung
                                         der Kerngarbe   C

[deep fire] … it cannot be called accident if the enemy is hit. By accident, I understand when at 2000 meters, a high, stray bullet hits a man. This is a chance hit. (Merkatz 1916: 53)

German experiments further determined that the total 'beaten zone' of the machine gun was only one-sixth the area covered by a similar number of rounds fired by the infantry. Moreover, not only did the fire of riflemen tend to disperse to a greater extent with increasing range, but the ability of the infantry to maintain a sustained effect was more limited; for even if riflemen were assured of a steady supply of ammunition, their ability to shoot accurately and rapidly gradually dropped off as they became tired. Conversely, being a machine, the MG 08 continued to shoot with much the same speed and effectiveness unless it actually suffered a mechanical stoppage, required a barrel change, or the crew were put out of action. The machine gun was, as one British commentator put it, 'nerveless'.

US and British tests simulating situations in which lines of riflemen were pitted against a Maxim gun at ranges from 600yd (550m) to 1,000yd (915m) demonstrated similar results, with the machine gun landing both an absolutely greater number of hits, and a higher percentage of hits from the total number of rounds fired. In most situations the smaller size of the machine gun when compared to a body of troops also counted as an advantage. Opinion varied as to exactly how many riflemen a Maxim was 'worth' in battle; numbers anywhere from 30 to as many as 120 are given in different contemporary authorities. In truth the balance must have been determined very much by the tactical situation, but almost always the machine gun outshot riflemen except at very close range.

When riflemen were advancing and machine guns well concealed, the verdict was often emphatic. As Georg Bucher saw at Fort Douaumont on the Verdun battlefield:

… the few hundred yards in front of Douaumont was an amazing sight. The dead, mostly German, lay in heaps. Then we came to a strip of ground where the French lay in rows and groups, the remains of a mass attack which had been repulsed; as they had moved forward, row after row, in waves of attack, they must have been mown down by the fire of cunningly sited machine gun nests. But where? I could see no signs of such strong points, and I was no longer sure of my direction in the bewildering labyrinth of trenches. (Bucher 2005: 43)

ROUNDS AND THEIR IMPACT

Bullets that 'expand or flattened easily in the human body' were banned specifically by the Hague Convention of 1899. At the same time Germany, like other countries, moved toward pointed bullets with metal jackets. These made best use of the power of the latest smokeless powders, and at the same time avoided shearing in the gun barrel and the heavy deposits to which relatively soft lead rounds were prone when subject to higher velocities. Though the German 'S', or pointed, 7.92mm rounds (also described in contemporary literature as 7.9mm) used during World War I were smaller and lighter than the unjacketed lead bullets current a few years earlier, there is no doubt that they were as effective, if not more so. This was not just because they were propelled by smokeless powder, worked more efficiently through the mechanism of a Maxim and more of them could be carried for the same weight, but because they lost little in terms of impact. They were faster, maintained a flatter trajectory for longer, and at the same time were less stable in their flight, despite the spin imparted by the rifling of the barrel. At over 3,800 joules the muzzle energy of the 1905 pointed round was about 25 per cent greater than its predecessor of 1888. True, some bullets passed cleanly through a limb or body without hitting anything vital, but any that were impeded were inclined to tumble, causing catastrophic injury and splintered bone. Moreover, though steel jacketed with a cupronickel coating, the bullet still had a lead core and deformed or broke apart when impacting anything sufficiently resistant.

During early demonstrations, Maxim cut down a tree with his gun, and this feat has been replicated recently with weapons using jacketed pointed rounds of the type current in World War I. This should not be too surprising, since the 7.92mm 'S Patrone' of the time had a muzzle velocity of approximately 878m/sec, and was capable of penetrating about 800mm of wood at close range. With human targets, 'through and through' penetrating wounds, with small entry holes and massive exit wounds, were commonplace. Depending on the angle of incidence and other factors, modern experiments show rounds creating a narrow channel, turning sideways, forming temporary cavities, and even flipping over to plough blunt end first through the target. Moreover, when a group target was particularly bunched it was perfectly possible for a single round to pass through more than one man. Bullets could also take odd courses through bodies, glancing off bone, or particularly at long range or when ricocheting, be stopped inside the victim.

An armour-piercing round, or 'K' bullet, known in German as the K-Munition, or SmK (*Spritz mit Kern*, 'pointed with core', or *Spritz mit Stahlkern*, 'pointed with steel core'), was introduced in 1915. This was identifiable by its slightly blunter point, a red-lacquer edging around the primer, and often a letter 'K' on the base. Packaging was also marked with a red 'K'. The core of these rounds was hardened steel set in lead, capable of penetrating about 12mm of armour plate at 100m, or 4.5mm at 900m, given a clean perpendicular strike. Initially, it was intended for dealing with steel loophole plates and other hardened targets, and could be shot at aircraft. It acquired another use with the advent of armoured warfare in 1916 as British Mk I and Mk II tanks were also flimsy enough to be penetrated.

'K' munition proved particularly important at Arras in April–May 1917, where a report from 27. Infanterie-Division opined that 11 April proved that rifle and machine-gun fire with armour-piercing ammunition could put tanks out of action, and was most effective when directed at their sides. At Bullecourt on 3 May it was indeed arguable that German Maxims and 'K' bullets determined the result of the action. Two tanks

attacking from the north had a tough time through gas and wire before armour-piercing bullets wounded both tank commanders, and several of the crew members. Both vehicles attacking in the centre were put out of action by various causes, and the two tanks to the south, and two in reserve, had little better success:

An MG 08 gun team of Königlich Sächsisches 5. Infanterie-Regiment *Kronprinz* Nr. 104, 1916. From this angle we see that the gun is fitted with the *Unterschild*, giving the firer partial protection from the front.

> Lt McCoull was temporarily blinded by concentrated machine gun fire on the front of the tank, and as far as is known drove into a trap consisting of a deep pit specially dug. Only one of the crew returned ... The other tank commander, Lt Knight, suffered heavy casualties on account of armour piercing bullets, and was unable to carry on fighting ... Meanwhile the remaining two tanks, under Lts Lambert and Smith, had moved up with an eye to exploitation but found this impossible. On reaching the outskirts of the village they were subjected to concentrated machine gun fire, and Lt Lambert and most of his crew were wounded, whilst in Lt Smith's tank an armour piercing bullet exploded the cordite of a six pounder shell, setting the tank on fire internally. Evacuation became necessary ... (Fletcher 1994: 37–38)

Other British reports noted that early tanks were particularly vulnerable at their ports and hatches, and in areas around the sponsons. The first French Schneider tanks were similarly susceptible to 'K' bullets, but from the spring of 1917 were fitted with improved armour to defeat the threat. The British Mk IV was likewise more heavily protected, and so the value of the 'K' round waned. Nevertheless, German literature continued to

71

promote its usefulness against tanks, and at Cambrai the SmK round was used in quantity; British tanks were engaged at close range, and there were successes.

Leutnant Kuhel of Reserve-Infanterie-Regiment Nr. 227 held the fire of his machine guns until the enemy were at 300m, then focused on a tank, 'sending showers of sparks in all directions' (Sheldon 2009: 98). The vehicle caught fire and suffered an explosion. Unteroffizier Hetschold of 1. Maschinengewehr-Kompagnie/Lehr-Infanterie-Regiment was closer still:

> I heaved my gun round and loaded 'K' ammunition. There was no time for thought; the monster was within 20 metres of me. I fired at the place where I had been taught. I could hear that my Gefreiter was also firing. There was a whirring noise and smoke appeared. Men jumped out of the monster and ran away. Driverless it came past us burning. It ran into a concrete block and jammed there. Just before that I saw my Gefreiter receive a direct hit, which hurled the machine gun up into the air. (Sheldon 2009: 114)

There were also complaints of inadequate supply of 'K' rounds, and its relative ineffectiveness against the latest armour, however. As Reserve Leutnant Dieckmann of Reserve-Infanterie-Regiment Nr. 19 recalled, 'some of our men were enraged when they realised our SmK ammunition and hand grenades were clattering uselessly against the armour' (Sheldon 2009: 166). In places supplies of the steel-cored rounds ran out entirely.

German 2. Armee instructions of 1918 were that 'K' rounds should be aimed primarily at vision slits and ports, and fired perpendicular to the armour of a vehicle to avoid bullets glancing off. A particularly worthwhile target was thought to be the right rear upper quarter of the Mk IV tank, from which the machine gun or marksman was less likely to suffer return fire. Armour-piercing ammunition had greater recoil than ordinary rounds, and full belts put a heavy strain on machine-gun springs and feed. As a result, when possible, specific weapons were fitted with stronger springs, and were marked out by means of a red ring painted around the barrel jacket. Belts for armour-piercing ammunition were sometimes also dyed red, and boxes marked with a 'K' (2. Armee 1918).

During the war German Maxims used an armour-piercing tracer cartridge, as well as a normal tracer round. These were put into belts of 'K' and 'S' cartridges respectively to allow the gun team to see where their shots were striking, and were particularly useful at night, against air targets, or where it was necessary to 'walk' fire onto the target. According to British intelligence the usual proportion of tracer in a belt was one in every ten rounds. A particularly unusual cartridge was the Patrone PrL, originally developed in 1916 for the destruction of observation balloons. This was an incendiary type with a filler of white phosphorus that burned during flight. Towards the end of the war a Patrone sS also made its appearance. Initially designed specifically for machine guns as a 'heavy pointed bullet', weighing 12.8g and identified by a green primer band, it was intended for long-range indirect fire.

A late-model MG 08/15 finishing a 250-round belt among a litter of spent cartridges, *c.*1939. In this view we can see how the new anti-aircraft sight is stowed on the side of the breech when not in use, as well as the position of the bipod near to the muzzle, adopted to improve stability and accuracy.

TACTICAL IMPACT

Vizefeldwebel Laasch of Reserve-Infanterie-Regiment Nr. 110 recalled an Entente attack on his position on the Somme in July 1916:

> Dense tightly packed lines poured out of the English trenches, strode across the wide foreground and ended up in the heavy defensive fire of regiment 180. I also fired one belt after another into the flank of the ever advancing English battalions with our machine gun: never in war have I experienced a more devastating effect of our fire; the fallen were tightly packed in the entire hollow up to Ovillers. However our machine gun had also been discovered. The last water had been poured into the jacket. We first noticed that the white steam had betrayed our position when individual gunshots went through our helmets or caused the sand to spray up in front of us. Now the shells swept into our trench from the left flank … (Quoted in Whitehead 2013: 261–66)

In the popular view the key tactical role of the MG 08, and indeed of machine guns in general in World War I, was to hold positions. They helped the defender to economize on troops, inflicting a terrible toll on those who attacked through trench lines and wire. As a US manual put it in 1917 when speaking of the Maxim, Vickers, Colt, Lewis and Hotchkiss alike:

> In trench warfare as it exists in Europe, automatic machine rifles, popularly called machine guns, find their greatest use. Besides the trench, the essential elements of a trench line consist of a depth of wire and a front of machine guns. The tremendous stopping power of machine guns enables them to replace a large number of riflemen along this line, reducing to a minimum the men employed in actual defense, thereby leaving a large part of the

force in reserve for use in a counter attack, or the assumption of the offensive at another part of the line. Their use also reduces the daily wastage due to sickness, and prevents the offensive spirit of the infantry from becoming impaired. (US War Department 1917a: 5)

Yet by the time this was written, German defensive methods had already moved on again, and again this was at least in part due to the MG 08 and the increasing distribution of the MG 08/15. Now German defences were progressively being organized not in lines, but in zones and webs of defence whose vital nodes were machine-gun positions providing interlocking fire. To many this is the fundamental point about the MG 08: that in concert with artillery and the trench it locked solid the front lines, particularly in the West. It prevented many a breakthrough and killed large numbers of Entente soldiers. Clearly this was often the case. However, this was not the only tactical significance of the Maxim in German hands, and arguably not even the most important. For the advent of a universal issue 'light' machine gun in the shape of the MG 08/15, and a reduction in the proportion of riflemen to machine-gunners, would alter the whole shape of both the infantry battle and infantry organization. In 1914, machine guns had been regarded as an augmentation to infantry firepower – an important addition in the shape of a 13th company to each infantry regiment. However, the degree of integration with riflemen was variable, and the ability of machine guns to move with infantry limited, particularly in the attack. Progressive increases in the numbers of machine guns, and the appearance of the MG 08/15 in particular, would change all this, so that by the end of the war infantry were often organized around the machine gun, rather than vice versa.

According to Hermann Cron, there were 18 times as many machine guns with the German Army at the end of the war as there were at the beginning; or, to put it another way, German machine guns had been employed at a density of approximately 3.5 per kilometre of the front during the Battle of the Marne in September 1914; around Rheims in 1918 there were 31 per kilometre, or an astonishing one piece for every 32m of front.

Initially, newly produced MG 08s went to top up shortfalls in existing front-line units, or to equip *Maschinengewehr-Kompagnien* for new units. By 1915 there were enough to start forming three- and four-gun *Feldmaschinengewehrzüge* (ad hoc machine-gun platoons) to bolster parts of the line. During 1916, infantry regiments themselves boasted oversized *Maschinengewehr-Kompagnien*, and some then formed a second company. Also, in January 1916 came the first *Maschinengewehr-Scharfschützen* units. These 'sharpshooters' drew initially on experienced machine-gun personnel who were sent to the machine-gun schools for an additional four- or five-week course. The skilled machine-gun units created had a higher level of knowledge and could be placed anywhere on the battlefield, either to focus fire 'offensively', often at longer ranges, or add a mass of fire to a defence. The *Maschinengewehr-Scharfschützen* personnel were identified by a badge depicting an MG 08, worn on the left upper arm.

During 1917 the pace of machine-gun expansion quickened as more and more MG 08/15s were added to the infantry. Cron notes a typical infantry regiment fighting in the West as receiving four MG 08/15s 'for training' in April 1917, with each infantry company being equipped with two guns in May. This was upped to four per company that September, and finally to six per company in February 1918. British intelligence was clearly interested in how issue was progressing, reporting in the summer of 1917 on prisoner information regarding Infanterie-Regiment *Graf Kirchbach* (1. Niederschlesisches) Nr. 46. Apparently the unit now possessed three machine-gun companies, each with nine MG 08 types; and no fewer than 45 light MG 08/15s were received on 13 June 1917, representing, it was thought, 'a complete issue of the new light machine gun' (General Staff 1917b: 3.16). This made a total of 27 MG 08s and 45 MG 08/15s for a three-battalion regiment fielding 12 rifle companies, and in point of fact there were more weapons yet to come.

Eventually there were, to put it mildly, Maxim guns everywhere. As Quartermaster General Erich Ludendorff explained, in the infantry company, 'the light machine gun had to become accepted as a normal part of the unit' (Ludendorff 2005: 574). Despite initial unfamiliarity, its firepower made it imperative that it became the 'main component' of the firefight. So it was that during 1917, in the West at least, each infantry company was allotted two, later four MG 08/15s. At first these were grouped together within the fourth platoon. This supported the other platoons which might themselves be designated as battle or assault platoons.

Subsequently, each platoon had its own light-machine-gun squad consisting of a leader and a four-man team to fire the gun and carry its ammunition, supported by four riflemen. Now it was possible to conduct fire and movement within a platoon, with the light machine gun providing suppressive fire and the other squads manoeuvring, perhaps to flank an enemy position before attacking with grenades, rifles and bayonets. Eventually, with dwindling numbers of men and increasing numbers of MG 08/15s, it even became possible to operate squads within which a four-man machine-gun section supported a larger number of riflemen. These mixed squads were described as *Einheitsgruppen*: 'unified' or 'standard' groups.

The direction of travel became even clearer when Ludendorff pronounced that when there were shortages of troops, those small units without a light machine gun should be the first to be disbanded, keeping as many machine guns with the front-line troops as possible. The war ended before the *Einheitsgruppen* could become universal, and the impact of the Armistice, the Treaty of Versailles and financial realities made sure that nothing of the sort could re-emerge formally in the 1920s – but by the 1930s small light-machine-gun squads and rifle squads again began to be integrated into 12- and 14-man units, each of which had a machine gun at its core.

An MG 08 team on a late 1930s field exercise. The gun mount is the interwar tripod as described in a publication of 1928 (Reichskriegsministerium 1928). This mount could also be used with an extension tube for anti-aircraft work.

CONCLUSION

The MG 08 and 08/15 were both typical weapons of their time, and which shaped their times. For while they were neither the first Maxims, nor arguably the technically most advanced Maxim designs, their impact on World War I and on the advance of infantry tactics was highly significant. In the first half of the war the most important role of the MG 08 was in holding the line, particularly when in 1915 or 1916 French or British attacks might have penetrated 'God's Wall' in the West. Increasingly subtle use, and increasing numbers of weapons, often made up for numbers of men, and ultimately also made it possible to economize on human life, and focus defence in 'webs'. Though Entente troops were rightly most wary of shelling, when the barrage stopped and men were out over the top it was

Inspection of an infantry platoon, 1936. The MG 08/15 is being used as a squad support weapon, pending large-scale issue of the new MG 34. The guns are fitted with blank-firing attachments and belt drums, and have their water pipes stowed wound around the barrel jackets.

the German machine guns that were quickest to focus on the threat.

We should not, however, fall into lazy thinking that because there were catastrophic occasions when whole battalions were halted by the MG 08, this was the only, nor even the most tactically significant, use of German Maxims. The German Army, and still more German arms manufacturers, were slow to develop and to produce the MG 08/15; but once they had done so, many new battlefield possibilities were revealed. First, the German soldier had something with which to counter the Lewis and other light machine guns and automatic rifles. Second, it made possible the projection of automatic fire with the assault; and as the MG 08/15 proliferated, in 1917 – and particularly during the first months of 1918 – platoons and finally squads could act in concert around the firepower of the light machine gun. Shock troops had a genuinely mobile support weapon, though still a fairly hefty one, and gains could quickly be occupied by a piece that had every prospect of repelling an enemy counter-attack.

A new term enters the German language: '08/15', or *Nullachtfünfzehn*, meaning 'general issue' or 'bog standard'. In the latter part of World War I the MG 08/15 was so familiar that its name became synonymous with 'commonplace'. The illustration is a flyer for the 1954 film, *08/15*, a drama written by Hans Hellmut Kirst and set at the beginning of World War II.

German instructions of 1917 and 1918 speak with much truth of an arm capable of lending 'moral' as well as tactical advantage to the front-line soldier. It also handed to the very small team, and even the individual gunner, a weapon that came close to making him master of his own destiny on the increasingly impersonal and inhuman battlefield. It was also a weapon with which he was expected to act with daring upon his own initiative. The way in which the MG 08/15 was used, and its acknowledged imperfections, would also inform the development of new generations of German machine guns after 1918. These became the ever more effective cornerstones of small-unit tactics; lighter and faster, arguably achieving what had been the holy grail of the *Einheitsmaschinengewehr* with the MG 34. Despite the interruption of Versailles, the goal of unified squads operating around a general-purpose machine gun was finally achieved, at least in the front-line infantry, just prior to World War II. Similar organizations were soon adopted by other major powers. Arguably, the echoes of the psychological impact of the *Nullachtfünfzehn* continue to be heard, even to this day.

BIBLIOGRAPHY

2. Armee (1918). *Merkblatt für Tankbekämpfung.* Zentralstelle d. Vermessungsdienst.

Applin, R.V.K. (1910). *Machine Gun Tactics.* London: Hugh Rees.

Bernhardi, Friedrich A.J. von (1899). *Unsere Kavallerie im nächsten Kriege.* Berlin: Mittler & Sohn.

Brose, Eric D. (2001). *The Kaiser's Army: the Politics of Military Technology in Germany during the Machine Age, 1870–1918.* Oxford: Oxford University Press.

Bruce, Robert (1997). *Machine Guns of World War I.* London: Windrow & Greene.

Bucher, Georg (2005). *In the Line.* Uckfield: Naval & Military Press.

Bull, Stephen (2007). *Stosstrupptaktik: German Assault Troops of the First World War.* Stroud: Spellmount.

Calef, John H. (1886). *Description and Service of Machine Guns.* Fort Monroe, VA: United States Artillery School.

Cornish, Paul (2009). *Machine Guns and the Great War.* Barnsley: Pen & Sword.

Cron, Hermann (2001). *Imperial German Army.* Solihull: Helion.

Feldman, Gerald G. (1992). *Army Industry and Labour in Germany 1914–1918.* Providence, RI: Berg.

Fletcher, David, ed. (1994). *Tanks and Trenches.* Stroud: Sutton.

General Staff (UK) (1911). *Tactical Principles for the Employment of Machine Gun Sections.* Translated from Austro Hungarian School of Musketry.

General Staff (UK) (no date). *Report on Foreign Manoeuvres in 1912.* Uckfield: Naval & Military Press.

General Staff (UK) (1914a). *Handbook of the German Army, 1912* (amended to August 1914).

General Staff (UK) (1914b). *Notes from the Front, Part 1.* London.

General Staff (UK) (1916a). *Lessons Drawn from the Battle of the Somme by Stein's Group.* Translation of a captured German document, SS480.

General Staff (UK) (1916b). *Order of the 6th Bavarian Division Regarding Machine Guns.* Translation of a captured German document, SS487.

General Staff (UK) (1916c). *Regulations for Machine-Gun Officers and Non-Commissioned Officers.* Translation of a captured German document, SS450.

General Staff (UK) (1917a). *Notes on Dealing with Hostile Machine Guns in an Advance.* SS155.

General Staff (UK) (1917b). *Summary of Machine Gun Intelligence, 1-3,* May–July 1917.

General Staff (UK) (1918). Notes on the 08 (Heavy) and 08/15 (Light) German Machine Guns. Translation of a captured German document, SS153.

Goldsmith, Dolf L. (1989). *The Devil's Paintbrush.* Toronto: Collector Grade.

Klaß, Major von, et al. (1915). *Der Gute Kamerad: ein Lern und Lesebuch.* Berlin: Liebelschen.

Kühlwein, Hauptmann (1934). *Felddienst ABC für den Schützen.* Berlin: Mittler.

Longstaff, F.V. & Atteridge, A.H. (1917). *The Book of the Machine Gun.* London: Rees.

Ludendorff, Erich (2005). *My War Memories.* Uckfield: Naval & Military Press.

Maxim, Hiram S. (1915). *My Life.* London: Methuen.

Merkatz, Friedrich von (1916). *New Methods of Machine Gun Fire.* Washington, DC: Infantry Association.

Merkatz, Friedrich von (1917 & 1918). *Das Maschinengewehr 08.* Berlin: Eisenschmidt. Editions of 1917 and 1918.

Musgrave, Daniel D. (1992). *German Machine Guns.* Revised edn. Alexandria, VA: Ironside International.

Nash, David, ed. (1977). *German Army Handbook April 1918.* London: Arms & Armour.

Patent Office (1993). *Patents for Inventions, Abridgement of Specifications, Class 119 Small Arms.* Oceanside, CA: Armory Publications.

Queckbörner, Hauptmann (1934). *Schiess ABC in Wort und Bild: EIn Illusttiertes Handbuch für das Schießen mit Gewehr und LMG 08/15, 08/18, und MG 13 (Dreyse) für Lehrer und Schüler.* Berlin: Mittler.

Reibert, Wilhelm (1933). *Die Maschinengewehre 08/15 und 08/18.* Berlin: Mittler.

Reichskriegsministerium (1911). *Feld-Pionierdienst aller Waffen.* DVE 275. Berlin: Mittler.

Reichskriegsministerium (1916). *Stellungsbau: The Construction of Field Positions.* English translation reprinted in *Trench Fortifications: A Reference Manual* (undated). Nashville, TN: Battery Press.

Reichskriegsministerium (1928). *Die Schießgestelle für MG 08.* Heeresdienstvorschrift 368. Berlin: Reichsdruckerei.

Reichskriegsministerium (1931). *Schießvorschrift.* Heeresdienstvorschrift 240. Berlin: Mittler.

Reichskriegsministerium (1937). *Schießvorschrift.* Heeresdienstvorschrift 73. Berlin: Mittler.

Reichskriegsministerium (1938). *Schulschießübungen für das Schießen mit dem Schweren Maschinengewehr.* Heeresdienstvorschrift 73. Berlin: Mittler.

Reichskriegsministerium (1940). *Ausbildungsvorschrift für die Infanterie, Teil 2.* Berlin.

Richter, Oliver (2012). *Grabenkrieg: German Trench Warfare, Vol. 2.* Erlangen: Jochen Vollert.

Schreibershofen, Max von (1914). *Die Modernen Waffen.* Leipzig: Kurt Stuck.

Sheldon, Jack (2005). *The German Army on the Somme.* Barnsley: Pen & Sword.

Sheldon, Jack (2009). *The German Army at Cambrai.* Barnsley: Pen & Sword.

Tilly, Feldwebel-Leutnant (1915). *Handbuch für das Maschinengewehr: MG Lehrkursus.* Döberitz.

Ulrich, Bernd, et al. (2010). *German Soldiers of the Great War: Letters and Eyewitness Accounts* (English translation). Barnsley: Pen & Sword.

US War Department (1917a). *Notes on the German Army in War.* Translated from a French document. Document 638. Washington, DC.

US War Department (1917b). *Notes on the Use of Machine Guns in Trench Warfare and on the Training of Machine Gun Units Compiled from Foreign Documents.* Document 580. Washington, DC.

US War Department (1918). *German Notes on Minor Tactics.* Translation of captured German documents, 1917. Document 713. Washington, DC.

Weber, Hauptmann von (1938). *Unterrichtsbuch für Soldaten.* Berlin: Offene Worte.

Whitehead, Ralph J. (2013). *The Other Side of the Wire, Vol. 2.* Solihull: Helion.

An MG 08/15 team from the latter part of the war. The gun kit includes no fewer than two oblong water cans and at least two different types of ammunition box. Close to the hand of the man on the left can be seen a spare gun lock. Three of the team have late-type web dragging straps, and at least five have the P 08 Luger pistol, a popular choice of back-up weapon for machine-gunners.

INDEX